Japan Unmasked

Japan
Unmasked

by

ICHIRO KAWASAKI

CHARLES E. TUTTLE COMPANY

Rutland, Vermont & Tokyo, Japan

Representatives

Continental Europe: BOXERBOOKS, INC., *Zurich*
British Isles: PRENTICE-HALL INTERNATIONAL, INC., *London*
Australasia: PAUL FLESCH and CO., PTY. LTD., *Melbourne*
Canada: M. G. HURTIG, LTD., *Edmonton*

Published by the Charles E. Tuttle Co., Inc.
of Rutland, Vermont and Tokyo, Japan
with editorial offices at
Suido 1-chome, 2–6, Bunkyo-ku, Tokyo

©1969, by Charles E. Tuttle Co., Inc.

Library of Congress Catalog Card No. 69–13500

First edition, 1969

Printed in Japan

Table of Contents

Author's Preface	*7*
A Nation of 12 Year Olds	*9*
Japanese Are Like That	*26*
Japanese Abroad	*44*
A Paradise for Foreigners	*59*
Metropolis to Megalopolis	*79*
Riding on a Career Escalator	*97*
Export or Perish	*113*
Hundred Million Customers	*131*
Once a Japanese; Always a Japanese	*151*

1868 and All That 170

Democracy—Japanese Style 184

"Coprosperity Sphere," Now and Then 202

Whither Japan 219

Author's Preface

CHERRY blossoms, geisha, and Mt. Fuji as symbols of Japan have, in recent years, largely given way to cameras, transistor radios, and supertankers. While the antiquated "image" of Japan still persists in many parts of the world, other nations are at last beginning to appreciate the tremendous strides Japan has made in her postwar rehabilitation and industrial expansion.

In fact Japan has risen from World War II shambles to fifth place among the world's industrial giants and, if the present trend is to continue, she will soon be the greatest industrial power second only to the United States. Already there is hardly a country in the world that is not affected by what Japan makes, buys, and sells today.

The asset of Japan as she moves into prominence

once again is not simply a matter of industrial statistics It is a tremendous national energy that within less than two decades has transformed a defeated, small, overcrowded island nation into one of the most dynamic industrial nations in the world.

But where is Japan going from here? What is the dream of the Japanese people? Will Japan be a major factor in the world's political scene? Will Japan emerge once again as a leading military power in Asia? These are some of the questions I have tried to answer in this little book. As a Japanese it has not been easy for me to be objective and conscientious. However, it is my firm conviction that mutual understanding among nations can best be promoted on the basis of candor and truthfulness, rather than by distortion and hypocrisy.

Nearly 13 years have elapsed since I first published *The Japanese Are Like That*. The original English edition has since been translated into Dutch and Portuguese. I realize that some of the facts and figures contained therein are getting somewhat out of date and feel that a completely new book on Japan and the Japanese may perhaps be in order.

Finally, I should like to add that the views expressed in this book are those of the author alone, and do not in any way reflect the views of the Foreign Office or the Japanese government to which I belong.

ICHIRO KAWASAKI

Warsaw, Poland

A Nation of 12 Year Olds

GENERAL of the Army Douglas MacArthur, who reigned supreme in Japan for seven years during the American military occupation of Japan, is said to have remarked once to the effect that the mentality of Japanese is that of a 12 year old.

This statement attributed to the late General MacArthur understandably gave rise to widespread resentment among the Japanese people and has been criticized even to this day. The former Supreme Commander for Japan evidently made this somewhat derogatory remark to a group of Americans in an off-the-record interview, but the unfortunate leak to the Japanese did much to detract from the popularity of the General. The average Japanese had looked upon MacArthur more as a benefactor than a conqueror, because of

9

a relatively benevolent occupation policy pursued by the United States vis-a-vis Japan.

Though the Japanese had suspected that General MacArthur was never very sanguine about the people over whom he ruled, judging by his deliberate effort at aloofness, the Japanese people felt quite chagrined and were flabbergasted when MacArthur made such an uncomplimentary remark about them. The Japanese people, however, never seem to have reflected why it is that a foreigner should make such an appraisal, or whether the Japanese deserved so scathing a verdict.

It is often the experience of a Westerner when he first goes to Japan to be bombarded with such questions as: "Have you seen Mt. Fuji?" or "Have you been to Nikko?" or "Have you seen a geisha?" etc. I have seen many a foreigner being asked such stereotyped questions by Japanese and I have often wondered why the Japanese should ask a newcomer such childish questions. The answer is simple.

In the first place, the command of the English language by the average Japanese is so poor that he cannot engage the stranger in a more elaborate exchange of views and ideas. The fact that Japanese are not good at foreign languages makes them feel all the more self-conscious and awkward in their contacts with foreigners. I have seen many foreign dignitaries visibly disappointed when they met leading personalities of the country on their visit to Japan. I myself have often been present or even acted as interpreter when distinguished visitors from abroad called upon prime ministers and other important personages of the country.

On such occasions the Japanese more often than not ask the callers perfunctory and stereotyped questions which are not at all conducive to animated or meaningful conversation. The main reason for this seems to be the language barrier, coupled with self-consciousness. For these same Japanese, when talking among themselves, have no inhibitions and are quite at ease and as intelligent and as versatile as they could possibly be.

Excepting a very few Japanese whose command of English is good and who possess a cosmopolitan background, foreigners generally find Japanese boring, especially on the first encounter. It is difficult for a foreigner to disarm the reserve and self-consciousness of the average Japanese. It takes quite some time to break the ice, and perhaps an evening of hilarious drinking is necessary to bring about the desired results.

Moreover, the Japanese generally like to stand on ceremony and indulge in expressions of curious condescension. Japanese, for instance, will say: "Please come to the dining room now, although there is nothing to eat." This is a very common Japanese expression, meaning that the food being offered is of no great value, though in actual fact the food is often very plentiful and sumptuous. Japanese humility and understatement is such that a Westerner may be taken aback, if invited to eat, when there is nothing to eat!

Coming back to the why and wherefore of the infantile conversation subjects, the Japanese, as a race, are a proud and dogmatic people. They are innocent enough to think, for instance, that Mt. Fuji is the most sublime peak in the world. I have,

11

however, seen similar symmetrically shaped vol-
canoes in other parts of the world, some perhaps
much higher, some even more grandiose and awe
inspiring. The Japanese logic is that since Mt.
Fuji is the most beautiful in the world, no foreigner
should fail to see it and, indeed, many foreign
visitors to Japan try to see the sacred mountain.

Geisha—woman entertainer-cum-hostess in a
teahouse—is a unique Japanese institution. In the
Japanese thinking, it would indeed be a pity if any
Westerner coming to Japan should miss the opportunity of meeting a geisha; however even if
they did, they certainly would not care to spend
the fantastic amount of money needed to hire one.

I myself, after having visited a number of foreign
capitals, know for a fact that Tokyo is one of the
ugliest and most disorderly capitals of the world,
though I admit that the city is rapidly being reno-
vated and provided with modern amenities. Yet
most Japanese honestly and truly believe that
Tokyo is a most wonderful city and that any
foreigner visiting there must be impressed by it.
Similarly, most Japanese think that a Westerner
is prejudiced against Japan mainly because he
does not know Japan and that if he sees the country for himself, he will surely become "pro-Japanese." While ignorance is partly responsible for
much of the Western bias against Japan and the
Japanese, it does not necessarily follow that all
foreigners who visit Japan will automatically come
to understand the country. However, this rather
naïve and, at the same time, dogmatic belief of the
average Japanese is so widespread that a large
number of foreigners each year are invited to visit

Japan, in many cases, with all expenses defrayed by Japanese government agencies, business firms, and even by private individuals.

Childishness of the Japanese people is most glaringly manifested in the blatant announcements often made over loudspeakers in public conveyances and other places in Japan. For example, on a long-distance train a loudspeaker announces to the passengers: "Next stop is Nagoya. The passengers leaving the train are kindly requested to make sure that none of their belongings are left behind," or "We apologize for the overcrowding of the train. Please beware of pickpockets while the train is in motion," etc. At a subway station in Tokyo a platform attendant will announce by means of a loudspeaker something like this: "This is Shibuya. Those bound for Shinjuku will please change trains by mounting the stairway right in front. Also may we remind you that there is a gap between the platform and the train coaches, so please be careful when alighting."

Such announcements sometimes can be helpful but more often than not quite uncalled for, and they often grate on one's nerves. The reasons for making such matter-of-fact announcements are many. The Japanese are courteous even to the point of being officious. Also, unbelievable congestion in public places makes it necessary to give such obvious reminders and warnings. At the same time, lack of individual initiative on the part of most Japanese and their tendency to act in mass psychology may, in part, be responsible for constantly telling others to do this and that.

Japanese are a good-natured people, presumably

because they have had little contact with aliens in their long history. Also having lived on their small islands in a frugal way with what little Nature could offer, Japanese are not rapacious by nature. But this good naturedness is sometimes carried to the extreme and no doubt gives the impression that the Japanese are a people of rather infantile mentality.

Recently a Japanese trading firm invited one of their British associates to visit Japan, as usual with all expenses paid by the host. While in Tokyo the visitor, a chronic diabetes patient, fell ill and was taken to a foremost hospital. Upon hearing the news, his wife, who happened to be in Australia at the time, flew to Tokyo to see her husband. In the meantime the hospital attendants had taken scrupulous care in their efforts to keep the patient on a strict diet. When the man's wife arrived and saw that he was craving certain things to eat, she gave them to him without the hospital attendants' knowledge. The patient's condition worsened, and he died. His wife then took issue with the hospital, and blamed the host company for failing to look after her husband properly while he was a guest in Japan. The company officials did not refute the allegation the woman had made, or even if they had, not sufficiently. The company, I hear, paid to this demanding woman a considerable amount of money as a solatium.

Side by side with good naturedness, emotionalism can also be cited as a characteristic of the Japanese people. The Japanese have been taught to remember indebtedness. If someone was kind to them at some time or other, the recipients of the kindness are expected not only to remember but also are expected to repay the kindness in some form or other whenever an opportunity presents itself. Apart from this sense of gratefulness, the Japanese are an extremely touchy people and are easily moved by emotionalism. When a Japanese athlete wins in some event in the Olympic Games, Japanese spectators almost always have tears in their eyes. When a Japanese team loses in some highly competitive game, the team members often weep and bewail themselves and make an emotional crisis out of it.

I still remember a pathetic scene at a railway station in Sendai many years ago when the American occupation came to an end. On the platform there were hundreds of young Japanese girls who had worked as maid-servants for the American occupation personnel's families of a military camp near the city. These girls were all in tears—weeping and sobbing and some were even wailing, as the American military train slowly pulled out of the station. None of the girls smiled at their former employers. It was a sad and tearful farewell bordering on a wake. In fact, just before the train departed, I saw on the platform not a few American housewives, gently patting the Japanese girls on the back, entreating them not to cry. It was like a mother trying to silence a crying baby. No wonder General MacArthur opined that Japanese had the mentality of 12 year olds.

Putting aside MacArthur for a moment, the Japanese as a whole feel a deep inferiority complex toward foreigners, especially Caucasians. However much the Japanese may disclaim this, an inferiority complex is so ingrained in their character that it often manifests itself in their daily life.

Recently my wife told me of her experience while traveling on a Japanese airliner bound for Europe. Sitting next to my wife, who is a native Japanese, was a European man who looked to her like an Englishman. A Japanese stewardess who was in charge of the cabin, made a point of offering drinks, food, and cigarettes to this European passenger first, and then to my wife. My wife told me that this gentleman himself was visibly embarrassed by the stewardess' unchivalrous etiquette. No wonder the Japanese airline advertises its "pampering" service. "Pampering" is all right, but it is limited to Caucasian passengers!

If a Japanese is accosted by a Westerner in the street and asked the way, the Japanese will often go out of his way to show the stranger how to get to his destination. This is an act of kindness that is appreciated in any country. But in other matters also, a Japanese accedes too readily to the wishes of a foreigner. A Japanese also gives in to a foreigner's threat too easily.

At the Tokyo Olympic Games held in 1964, the French contingent of athletes arrived in Japan, and upon arrival was handed a program of various events printed in English by the organizers of the Games, the Japanese National Committee for the Olympic Games. But the French athletes refused to accept the program on the ground that it was not written in French, the "international" language. Now it is well known that Frenchmen have been in the habit of using the French language as a lever to enhance their national prestige whenever practical. In fact it seems to be their national policy to do so.

The Japanese Olympic officials, at the protest of the French athletes, tendered deep apologies and hurriedly went to the trouble of translating the entire program into French, and had it printed and distributed to the French visitors. I do not know whether such a regulation exists within the Olympic Committee in regard to the printing of programs in both French and English, but even if there were, if the same incident happened in other countries, officials of the countries concerned would surely ignore the protest as unwarranted. After all, it was a trivial matter which merely related to the program and any Frenchman could very well have read or understood it. I even doubt if the Frenchmen would have refused to accept the program in English if the same thing had happened in Europe or America. The Japanese good naturedness is such that it is often taken advantage of by other peoples and, in many such cases, the Japanese must give the impression of being quite childish.

The Japanese tend to believe wholeheartedly what foreigners, especially Occidentals, tell them or what they have to say. Hence a Japanese scholar, when writing a thesis, quotes freely from Western writers in order to make his thesis appear more authoritative. A Japanese lecturer tells an audience that an American or European authority has said such and such a thing in order to substantiate his point of view.

Since the end of the war, the Japanese generally

have less regard for and are little interested in the emperor either as a person or as an institution. But a few years ago when a British journalist published a book on the present Emperor Hirohito, and when the Japanese translation of the book was published soon afterward, the book became one of the best sellers in Japan. The contents of the book were nothing new to the Japanese, but the fact that a Westerner had written a book on the emperor of Japan was enough to impress the Japanese reading public and to revive their interest in the emperor.

Certain Japanese newspapers have special arrangements with the *Times* of London or the *New York Times,* whereby they are authorized to reprint some of the articles appearing in those papers. Of course the Japanese newspaper companies have to pay huge sums for such services, but it nevertheless is the best way to promote newspaper sales. The Japanese reading public places more value on reports appearing in the British or American papers than on those emanating from their own Japanese correspondents stationed in London or New York. Such credulity of the Japanese may be due to various factors, such as their blind reverence of things Western and their inferiority complex toward Occidentals, but it also betrays their rather infantile mentality.

The Japanese have not yet been able to develop individualism as it is understood in the West. They have been used to repressing their own ego in their relations to the family or community. Thus, a Japanese individual can be said to be devoid of backbone, so to speak. He is pliant, has no firm convictions of his own, and tends to act with group psychology. This is the reason why a Japanese, when he goes to a Western country for the first time, often falls in love with the country to a remarkable degree. Many Japanese who resided in France for any length of time have, in many cases, become Francophilic. I have known many such Japanese who take inordinate pride in speaking French, singing French *chansons,* and wearing beret Basque caps even after they come back to Japan. People like the French who have a strong individual character, seem particularly to appeal to the Japanese, whose life has always been fettered by numerous social strictures and inhibitions.

Hence the Japanese, when they go to a Western country like France, at last breathe the air of freedom which they have never experienced before, so much so, that they readily take to the way of life of the country. Many of my colleagues who had been stationed in England likewise became so enamored of the English way of life that some of them even continue to wear a bowler hat, read the *Times* of London, and carry an umbrella regardless of the weather, after returning to Japan. And, they will probably continue to do so for the rest of their lives.

In Japan there is some sort of craze, or what the Japanese call a "boom," that strikes the whole nation from time to time like an epidemic. There has, for example, been a craze for growing orchids, for collecting old coins, for owning Western antique furniture, etc. Recently there was a boom for collecting stones and rocks, large and small, mainly for ornaments, when most well-to-do frantically went in for all sorts of stones, curiously shaped or fantastically colored. As a result, there developed a big market for stones not only for business but also for speculation. It is characteristic of these fads, however, that they are usually not sustaining and once the craze is over, everybody completely forgets about it as if nothing had happened, much like a calm morning after a stormy night.

If someone starts doing something out of the ordinary, his fellow countrymen find it difficult to resist the temptation not to follow suit, and in fact, the whole nation succumbs to the fad. The absence of a strong ego with the Japanese is also responsible for the Japanese penchant for imitating indiscriminately what others, especially Westerners, do or say.

This Japanese "selflessness" may in part account for the recent corruption of the Japanese language with English words. Everywhere in Japan today one catches the sound of English words—in the jargon of politics, in the language of trade and technology, clothes fashions, magazine titles, foods, and sports. For instance, *mudo* for English mood, is a word which might seem a little odd but everyone can at least guess the meaning. *Mudo* is increasingly used in daily conversations as well as in advertisements. An advertisement for a high-class apartment house in Tokyo says that "the *manshon* (mansion) is *hai kurasu* (high class) and *gojasu* (gorgeous)." Mansion, high class, and gorgeous are all English words adopted into the Japanese language with somewhat perverted meanings. A man may take a *takushi* (taxi) to go to *resutoran* (restaurant) and have *hamu raisu* (ham rice), a favorite Japanese dish consisting of boiled rice mixed with chopped ham and green peas. They are pretty accurate and certainly uninhibited approximations. No danger of mispronunciation confronts the Japanese, for they think in syllables and everything can be transliterated into the relatively simple Japanese *katakana* syllabary.

Though most of these adopted English words have exact approximations in the Japanese language, the Japanese, due to their passionate love of things Western, are mutilating their own language by adopting more and more English words—mostly nouns—almost indiscriminately. There reigns a veritable babel of confusion in the Japanese language today as a result of this totally uncalled-for adoption of English words, to the utter despair of purists and conservatives. The Japanese have in their long history never had much genuine pride in their own culture, which in itself is a borrowing or adoptation of Chinese and other foreign cultures. This selflessness, coupled with their avid curiosity for things Western, has resulted in this lamentable mutilation of their own language. To a Western observer this craze for English words may appear to be another instance of Japanese imbecility.

It is well-nigh impossible to keep secrets in Japan today. For this, the lack of the Western concept of individualism among the Japanese is largely responsible. Information of a confidential nature is easily passed on since the individual concerned is simply unable to resist the temptation of giving away the information to someone else. The Japanese ego is weak. In the absence of any legislation penalizing the dissemination of important state secrets, there is nothing in Japan today which prevents confidential information from being leaked to whomever is fishing for such.

Soon after the surrender of Japan in August, 1945, General MacArthur arrived in Japan and set up his headquarters in Yokohama. The General Headquarters had prepared a proclamation to introduce a direct military rule, including the use of military scrip in lieu of Japanese yen, and the setting up of military courts all over the country. The Japanese government had heard of the project and was very perturbed over the possible effects of the proposed measures on the populace.

Thereupon, high government officials made an eleventh-hour appeal to MacArthur not to introduce such harsh measures for fear that they might antagonize the Japanese. MacArthur acceded to the Japanese government's plea, and direct military rule was forthwith rescinded at his own discretion. The negotiations had of course been conducted in strict secrecy, but in no time the information was leaked to the press and was even reported to the United States by American correspondents. The American government was said to have been displeased over the liberty taken by the General to modify the original occupation directives, especially in deference to the Japanese wishes. It has been said that General MacArthur was mildly rebuked. I heard that the General at the time confided to one of his aides that he was so disgusted with Japanese ministers' inability to guard secrets that he henceforth would receive no one from the Japanese cabinet. During the seven years following that incident he indeed never once again received any of the Japanese cabinet ministers.

While Japanese traditionally are friendly, generous, and patient and do not lack in intelligence, they often betray immaturity in their thinking. The fact that Japan had been cut off for centuries from the outside world accounts for the lack of confidence on the part of Japanese in their dealings with other peoples. As a people nurtured in the isolated surroundings of their small islands and having had little contact with foreigners, the Japanese are good natured and tend to think of other peoples in terms of their own. The Japanese are often swayed by emotion and harp on vague generalities and are apt to lose sight of realities.

This immaturity is particularly noticeable in the realm of Japanese diplomacy. In order to gain popularity among the electorate, Japanese politicians play up Japan's role in the world as being important and even decisive, which, however, is not substantiated by facts. The majority of the Japanese do think and hope that Japan should by now be playing a leading part in Asia, at least, and government leaders come out with high-sounding slogans such as "activization of Japan's Asian diplomacy," in order to pander to popular demands. These slogans, not being backed by Japan's own actions or capabilities, sooner or later die a natural death. There is a curious mixture of wishful thinking and aspiration which betrays the immaturity of the Japanese mind.

Coming back to General MacArthur once again, it must not be forgotten that he was ruling a

23

country whose people were laid prostrate by their defeat in the war. Japan had never before in her long history been beaten in a foreign war; the country's geographical position is such that it had been singularly free from foreign invasion. In the 12th century the Mongol hordes tried to invade Japan by deploying a large force, but they were thwarted in the adventure by a storm which broke out over the Straits of Korea, which is ten times the width of the Straits of Dover. In the wake of the Pacific War then, Japanese sense of security and invincibility was rudely shattered by their disastrous defeat, and the loss of confidence in themselves was complete.

Under these circumstances the Supreme Commander of the American occupation forces had an exceedingly easy task and encountered no resistance at all from any quarter. To the Japanese it was as though their emperor, to whom they had owed absolute allegiance, was suddenly replaced by General MacArthur. It was said in the early days of the occupation that a crying child was lulled to silence when told that an American soldier was around. During the occupation I once saw a huge crowd gathering in front of a theater in a remote provincial town. There was a big sign board reading "All Nude Show by the special permission of the Occupation Forces."

It was easy to see that whenever General MacArthur talked to a Japanese there was no dissenting voice. He was always met by the Japanese, who merely nodded an assent, even when his directives or suggestions seemed high handed and unreasonable. The General might well have concluded that the Japanese were a childish people who were incapable of talking back or asserting their rights.

Almost 15 years after the end of the occupation, the Japanese are at last beginning to feel, in a vague way, that theirs after all is not a nation to be ashamed of, and attention is once again being focused on "Japan" as the central value of the Japanese. But there is as yet no precise indication as to what in or about Japan is to serve as a national goal.

There was the time immediately following the surrender when the hoisting of the rising sun national flag was deemed an undesirable and even shameful act. In fact, any symbols of Japan were discarded *in toto,* including singing of the national anthem. The reawakening of nationalism in post-war Japan, however, is not likely to lead to the resurgence of the extreme right wing as was the case in prewar years. The popular Japanese mood is too pacifist to allow the rightists to assert themselves.

Today many Japanese are still dubious about the extent of their own achievements and capabilities, and are convinced that the West is superior to them in many ways. But the Japanese will gradually regain the confidence which was shattered by their disastrous defeat in the war, thereby attaining greater maturity in their conduct as well as in their thinking.

Japanese Are Like That

OF ALL THE races of the world, the Japanese are perhaps physically the least attractive, with the exception of Pygmies and Hottentots. Members of the so-called Mongolian race to which Japanese belong, have flat expressionless faces, high cheek bones, and oblique eyes. Their figure is also far from being shapely with a disproportionately large head, an elongated trunk, and short, often bowed legs.

Compared with Japanese, Chinese and Koreans, who are physiognomically very akin to the Japanese are, if anything, taller and straighter. In fact the Japanese have been referred to as dwarfs from time immemorial in China. The history of East Asia, notably that of China and Siam, records many instances of assaults by Japanese pirates on their shores, and the Japanese marauders were invariably called *wako,* or dwarf pirates. Today Europe is linked directly with Japan by air over the North Pole, and a tourist arriving in Tokyo directly from Europe is forcibly reminded that Japan is indeed a land of Liliputs. Indians and Pakistanis, too, are called Asians but they are of Aryan origin and while they, too, suffer from inferiority complexes toward the whites, they themselves tend to look down on the Japanese as being physically less attractive than themselves. Much has been said in recent years about apartheid. Negroes in America and black Africans in South Africa are the targets of racial discrimination and even persecution. But even Negroes, their pigmentation of skin notwithstanding, are at least taller and straighter than the Japanese and perhaps have a greater sex appeal.

The Japanese, both men and women, generally look much younger for their age than do Westerners. In fact foreigners often complain of the difficulty in telling the age of Japanese. The fact that Japanese, and East Asians for that matter, have rather flat and boyish faces, makes them look a good deal younger than Caucasians of the same age. Also the fact that Japanese have been non-meat eaters for many centuries may be responsible for their rather youngish looks. The Japanese are not generally precocious and do not reach maturity as quickly as Westerners. Another reason for the youthful appearance of the Japanese, I believe, is psychological. Under the influence of Buddhism, which has taught Japanese to be modest in their desires and acquisitions, Japanese people, like some other Asians, are generally happy-go-lucky and this may partly account for the Japanese not aging too quickly. Generally speaking, if a Westerner wants to know the correct age of a Japanese, he is well advised to add ten years to what appears to be the age of the Japanese. However, the Japanese among themselves, can almost infallibly tell the other's age.

The Japanese have improved their physique somewhat in recent years, due to a better and more balanced diet and also as a result of a change in their mode of living; in particular, a greater use of chairs in their living quarters. Statistics show that the average Japanese youth today is taller by three centimeters and his weight and chest measurements have increased correspondingly, compared with his counterparts at the end of the war. However, due to great congestion in their living space and, above all, on account of the almost inhuman cramming ordeal to which most school children are subjected in order to get into the higher seats of learning, the majority of Japanese youths have neither the time nor access to facilities to develop their physique properly. Hence it is likely that the Japanese will continue to be a physically inferior race for many years to come.

This physical inferiority, coupled with the fact that Japanese belong to the yellow race, has destined the Japanese to be the outcasts, so to speak, of the world. Bismarck sounded a warning to the world by conjuring up the specter of "yellow peril" at the turn of the century when a tiny Japan emerged victorious over the colossus of Tsarist Russia, in the wake of the Russo-Japanese War of 1904–5. When Japanese emigrants began pouring into the United States at the beginning of the century, the state of California enacted the Japanese Exclusion Act, whereby the Japanese immigrants were placed on a negligible quota, and Japanese immigration into California was virtually outlawed. Some Japanese historians maintain, perhaps with reason, that this very act of discrimination against Japanese as an undesirable racial group by the Americans, had driven Japan on the path of armed expansion on the Asiatic continent, culminating in the Pacific War.

Of late a number of Asian and African nations have been clamoring for the abolition of racial discrimination in the United Nations and on other international forums. In particular, apartheid, as practiced by South Africa, has been a target of vehement attack by Afro-Asian peoples. Few, if any, remember today that it was Japan that appealed for the racial equality at the Versailles Peace Conference of 1918, which brought World War I to a close. The Japanese proposal was not carried by the conference but it was certainly a forerunner of what was to come. World opinion seems to have been sufficiently aroused to the injustice and immorality of racial discrimination.

Under constant pressure from the colored races, the situation is expected to improve as time goes on. However, with human nature being such as it is, one cannot be too optimistic. Racial prejudice is so ingrained in the minds of the peoples of the white race that no early solution to the problem appears in sight. In such circumstances it is my belief that the Japanese people, despite their intelligence and capabilities, have been seriously handicapped in their dealings with the West and will find it forever difficult to compete on a completely equal footing with the West.

I once knew an Englishman, a retired merchant marine captain, who lived in Yokohama, Japan. He was married to a Japanese woman who hailed from a respectable family. This British friend used to tell me that just because his wife was Japanese, he was ostracized by the local British community and was obliged to live a rather solitary life outside his own community.

While it is undeniable that there is a latent dislike and even hostility on the part of many Caucasians toward Japanese, this racial prejudice is much less in evidence when youngsters of the East and West are involved. Children the world over are jovial, nonchalant, and are good mixers. As they grow older and their vital interests become at stake, Caucasians more often than not start discriminating against non-Aryan peoples.

A Japanese friend of mine who once lived in Berlin, Germany, had this heart-rending experience. My friend's daughter used to go to a German school. She spoke German like a native and had no difficulty either in her studies or in mixing with her German classmates. One day this Japanese girl came home during school hours in tears. When she saw her mother, she began sobbing and said she would never again go back to her school. She told her mother that she had been discreetly excluded from a party to which all her German friends were invited.

An increasing number of Japanese musicians in

recent years have participated in various international festivals and contests, and not a few distinguished themselves. A few years ago in Warsaw, Poland, a Japanese girl won fourth place in the Chopin Piano Contest which is held every five years and is rated as one of the foremost piano contests of the world. Over 200 talents from all over the world took part in the competition and were eliminated in three different rounds until 6 winners were finally chosen. This young Japanese girl was quite popular at the beginning as a petite, exotic talent among both the competitors and the audience. She told me that as the contest wore on, Caucasian participants became less cordial, and someone in the audience tried to jar her nerves while she was playing by sounding an alarm clock, and some even jeered. She later confided to me that never had she been so forcibly reminded of the well-known adage that ". . . East is East, West is West, and never the twain shall meet."

Such instances of racial discrimination, both overt or otherwise, are unfortunately too numerous when Japanese abroad are concerned. Birds of a feather flock together, the saying goes and it is perhaps human nature that a Caucasian man would rather like to mix with his own folk and does not like, for instance, to be seen dancing with a diminutive Japanese girl. Nor does the fault lie entirely with the Caucasians. The average Japanese is as yet, socially, not quite used to Western habits and customs. A Japanese man or woman often cuts a forlorn figure in the company of Westerners. Japanese, even in these days of jet travel with their ever increasing contact with the West, behave awkwardly and unnaturally in the company of foreigners, so ingrained is their insularity. At the same time it still is a severe strain on many a Japanese to mix with foreigners.

The dinners and receptions given by Japanese embassies abroad are, needless to say, exceedingly lavish affairs, Western or Japanese style. Such expensive dishes as *pâte de fois gras,* for instance, are served without stint, while French champagne of old vintage is freely imbibed. The Japanese, by such extravagant acts, feel that they can make up for their poor performance as conversationalists. At a dinner party to which Westerners are invited, the Japanese host and hostess are usually unable to engage the guests in animated talks, due largely to their poor command of English or French and also to their innate shyness. As a result, a Japanese dinner party often degenerates into a quiet and solemn affair bordering on a wake. In such situations perhaps the only way to satisfy the guests is to make the menu more attractive. It is also in conformity with Japanese hospitality that when one invites others, one is supposed to give the very best in the way of food and drink without regard to the cost. Such extravagant entertaining is also common among the Chinese, Indonesians, and other Asians.

Foreign embassies in Tokyo try to invite Japanese people to dinners and other functions, but they often complain of difficulty in getting the right type of Japanese who can mix freely with foreigners. I have often seen at a formal dinner a Japanese lady sitting immobile, responding to conversational gambits of Westerners who sit next to her, with an agonized "yes" or "no," counting the minutes until she can return to her home. It is the fate of the Japanese that they will continue to be treated as social outcasts for many years to come. This is a deplorable fact, but it nevertheless has to be taken into consideration whenever one discusses Japan's place in the comity of nations.

Going back to the physical and other characteristics, it is noteworthy that homosexual cases among the Japanese are relatively few. London and other Western cities abound in certain kinds of clubs, shops, and newsstands with pornographic publications which clearly testify to the prevalence of this abnormal sex propensity. The Japanese, both men and women, are comparatively free from this abnormity, presumably because they have lived a rather natural life from their childhood in the matter of food, clothing, and living quarters which are free of repression. However, it may be that with Japanese ways of living becoming more tense and sophisticated, this sexual perversion may well become more rife.

The Japanese are known to have a somewhat lower body temperature than Occidentals, due presumably to a lower intake of animal protein. Their average body temperature is around 37 degrees centigrade or less. As a consequence, the Japanese stand the cold much less easily than Westerners. I once saw a young Japanese traveler who tried to swim in the Lake of Geneva. After an initial dip of a few minutes, this man came out of the water shivering terribly, his lips turning purple! The water temperature at the time was 19 degrees centigrade, which is quite comfortable to a Westerner. A few years ago an intrepid Japanese college student tried to swim across the English Channel, but had to give up the attempt because the water was too cold for him.

The fact that most Japanese men wear warm underwear is due in part to their body temperature. This habit is so ingrained that some Japanese men wear knee-length underwear all the year round, even in summer. The reason for wearing this apparel in summer, however, may be due to their desire to protect their trousers from perspiration, for the summer in Japan can be very sultry. It is for this practical purpose that Japanese men wear under their trousers a thin, white garment called *suteteko,* much like the bottom half of pajamas. Japanese gentlemen are often seen nonchalantly shedding trousers on trains and remaining seated in their *suteteko*—much to the utter consternation of foreign female passengers. This garment has been in use for many years, and Japanese men used to lounge in these thin pants in places other than train seats long before Western trousers were adopted.

Japanese hair, both male and female, is jet black. It is a remarkable fact that there is no exception whatsoever, which speaks for homogeneity of the Japanese people. The Japanese, however, adore blond, ginger, brown, or any other color of hair but black, so much so that one often sees Japanese men and women dying their hair. Japanese hair is also coarse and brittle. Particularly is this the case with men's hair, and for a Western barber it is sheer terror to cut Japanese men's hair which is as hard as brush bristles. An Occidental barber is often visibly annoyed by the quality of the Japanese men's hair, and the Japanese are conscious of this fact. The latter therefore tip the Western barber most generously in order to curry favor or, at any rate, to mitigate the displeasure of the hairdresser.

The average Japanese is not hairy; their arms and chest are smooth and usually devoid of hair. Rarely does one find a hairy man. A man with hair on his chest is often the idol of Japanese women. What hairy Japanese there are, are usually descendents of Ainu, the semi-Caucasian tribe of northern Hokkaido which is practically on the verge of extinction today.

A Japanese with a cold, or one who suspects that a cold may be imminent, clamps a white gauze pad over his nose and mouth, and attaches it by elastic loops around his ears. These gauze pads, worn mostly in winter, which may look quite outlandish at first sight, are as common as kimono and attract no more attention on a busy Tokyo street than an umbrella does on Bond Street. This ungainly mouth cover is the remnant of a worldwide epidemic of Spanish influenza of the 1910's, which also raged in Japan. The Japanese still find this particular type of mouth cover a convenient way to avoid contact with germs in crowded places, and it is also worn so as not to annoy others with one's sniffles.

The Japanese show considerable bashfulness in exposing their naked body. This may sound contradictory to their well-known habit of going to a communal bath. However, the Japanese are not exhibitionists. In a public bathhouse, a Japanese

35

man or woman, once undressed, carries a small hand towel with which he or she tries to conceal the vital parts as much as possible. This small towel may also be used in place of a sponge or wash cloth when bathing.

Westerners meet in a shower room stark naked without trying to hide their reproductive organ, as if it were like any other part of their body such as the nose or ears. Such a practice is strange, if not horrifying to the Japanese, and also to Asians in general to whom nudity is disgusting. I once heard a Pakistani student in New York remark that it was a most serious ordeal for him to swim in a certain YMCA pool where the regulation provided for not using swim trunks. He abhorred the practice as barbarian.

In India millions of pilgrims go to Benares to bathe in the sacred waters of the River Ganges. To an orthodox Hindu this is a great event. I once watched them bathing in the river. A pilgrim dips into the water wearing a kind of loin cloth. When he emerges from the "holy" water he naturally has to remove this apparel. I was amazed to see how dextrous a Hindu can be in removing the dripping wet garment, just at the moment when he changes into a dry one. He never for a moment allows himself to be exposed. Asians, including Japanese, are most anxious to observe this decorum, and go to great lengths in their effort not to expose their vital parts in the presence of others.

The Japanese, as an individual, is a small feeble creature. Man for man the average Japanese is no match for a Westerner. Physically, the Japanese has no stamina or energy comparable to that of a

Caucasian. This is evidenced by the fact that at International Olympic Games Japanese athletes find it well-nigh impossible to distinguish themselves in those games which require sheer physical superiority. It is only in such sports as gymnastics or table tennis, for instance, in which skill or dexterity plays a more decisive role, that the Japanese sportsmen emerge in anyway victorious.

Individual achievements of the Japanese people have generally been meager. Despite the highly advanced technological standard of the country, few Japanese have attained international fame either as scientists or scholars. Not that there have never been outstanding savants or scientists among the Japanese, but the results of their studies have not always received wide publicity or recognition, due to the language difficulty and also to the isolated geographical position of the country.

Japanese artists and painters have produced many exquisite objects of art from time immemorial. Yet their works, however refined and artistic in their own way, are nowhere comparable to the great arts of the West. Water-color drawings of flowers, birds, and mountains—the themes favored by the old Japanese masters—are usually delicate and frail, and not half as powerful or demonstrative as the immortal works of Michelangelo or Rembrandt.

I have explained elsewhere how poverty has molded the Japanese character in more ways than one. As a corollary to this, mention must also be made of the Japanese capacity to find contentment in small things. In a country where scantiness of resources is the order of the day, a Japanese has always considered himself lucky if he did not starve. Nor has it been easy to amass a great fortune in a country which is lacking in natural resources and which had been cut off from the outside world. What riches Japanese feudal lords could amass, and more recently the wealth Japanese industrial-ists and businessmen enjoy, are paltry compared with those of their Western counterparts.

Apart from the physical limitations of Japan, religion is also responsible for the Japanese being modest in their quest for material gains. Accord-ing to Buddhist teachings, the way to happiness in yonder life is to be modest in want in the pres-ent life. For centuries, Japanese have respected the warrior class more than any other and looked down upon the merchant class as a less desirable vocation. In feudal times even farming was con-sidered a superior calling to merchandising. Though Japanese business and trade developed early and there existed various commodity ex-changes as early as the 16th century in Tokyo (Edo) and Osaka, it was not until recently that trade and commerce began to assume paramount impor-tance.

This comparative freedom from greed may also arise from the fact that Japanese have not been meat-eaters. It is obvious that a people subsisting on rice, fish, and vegetables are by nature less de-manding and less voracious than a meat-eating race. Mahatma Ghandi was, throughout his life, content with a bare minimum of food and cloth-ing, and conducted a great spiritual movement in India. He was a strict vegetarian. Ghandi prop-agated a line of non-violence in order to attain independence for India. Despite an outward appearance of affluence and prosperity in Japan today, this freedom from greed still is a dominant trait of the Japanese. This is not to say that Japanese do not rob or swindle others. Unfortunately there are as many such crimes perpetrated in Japan as in other countries. Still, malicious murders and sensational kidnappings are perhaps less numerous in Japan than in some Western countries. Japanese newspapers report almost daily of honest taxi-drivers who try to locate the passengers who have left money or other valuables in their cabs.

As an individual a Japanese does not appear to be particularly efficient. A visit to a Japanese government office or business firm will give that impression. In particular, the Japanese seem to lack initiative. They are often muddled and at a loss in cases where a precedent has not been set. Nor do the Japanese seem to work particularly hard and intensively. One often sees them whiling away their time, sipping tea or gossiping. Visitors, including friends and relatives, are ushered into the office and engaged in prolonged conversations which do not relate to business. At any rate the Japanese do not concentrate on their work during the specified working hours as do people in the West.

For in Japan the concept of a man's relationship to his job is entirely different from that of the West. To the Western worker, the job is an instrument for the enrichment and satisfaction of the real part of his life, which exists outside the place of work. For the Japanese worker, life and job are so closely interwoven that it cannot be said

39

where one ends and the other begins. So if a Japanese office worker has some unfinished work, he will stay in the office after closing hours until he finishes, without asking for overtime payment. Other workers actually take the work home to do after dinner or even on Sunday!

Despite all these apparent signs of inferiority and weakness, Japan has become one of the world powers and, even after the disastrous defeat in the war, has achieved something truly phenomenal in her postwar rehabilitation. Astonishing bursts of economic activity in recent years is a matter of genuine wonderment to the rest of the world, which still tends to underestimate Japan's ability and her achievements. Why is it then, that when the Japanese as a whole are capable of such miraculous economical advances, as individuals they are neither very efficient nor particularly energetic? The answer for this seemingly inexplicable phenomenon lies in what I would call anonymous and collective activity of the Japanese people.

I have pointed out how the Japanese think and act collectively. The Japanese as an individual may not work as intensively as a Westerner, but the sum total of all their work may perhaps be much greater than the work done by the same number of Westerners. For one thing, the Japanese worker normally does not take a prolonged holiday. To be sure, a Japanese civil servant is assured a two-week paid holiday every year, but few, if any, dare to take this officially stipulated leave in full, for fear that their colleagues may think ill of them as being selfish or frivolous. At most they will take only a few days off and then work for the rest of the year without grumbling. The Western notion of right and duty has never been firmly ingrained into the Japanese mind. Also a very severe competition for survival among the Japanese is responsible for their reluctance to take their quota of annual leave.

Thus the Japanese, taken as a whole, work longer hours and, perhaps, with greater results. Also strikes and other labor disputes, though they may often be reported in the newspapers, are much less frequent than in the West. Japanese workers are known to resort to their so-called summer and winter offensives to demand an increase in their semi-annual bonus payments. These are token strikes and both union leaders and the employers invariably end up in a suitable compromise when the time comes. So these strikes cannot be regarded as labor strikes in the strictest sense of the term.

Japan's industrial power is rather differently based from that of Western industrial countries. It does not rely on great natural resources or enormous capital reserves. The power comes from a large and hard-working labor force backed by devotion to work, ingenuity in methods, and clever management. Labor in a throbbing industry is not just mere work. Also there is a built-in collectivism in the Japanese people. Like so many other things in Japan, work is a ceremony, and this feeling for ceremonies and rites creates in nearly all factories and workshops a feeling of kindness and respect for human dignity.

The directors of most Japanese factories usually provide free lessons in flower arrangement, the tea ceremony, Japanese music and dance, baseball, judo, and other sports for their employees. These fringe benefits please the workers and contribute to their harmonious relationship. Also, the tea ceremony and other such Japanese pastimes seem so essential for the health and peace of mind of the workers who have to toil in the infernal racket of engine rooms and tolerate the slogging heat of blast furnaces.

Japanese workers gather on factory grounds and engage in calisthenics before starting the day's work. They are cheerful and humor is always present. For instance, when someone gets confused and starts bending in the wrong direction, laughter and smiles flit throughout the factory and pervade in the workshop for the rest of the day. Factories in Japan thus cater to the Japanese taste for some kind of regimentation and formal order, thereby fulfilling the Japanese yearning to "belong." In many factories such as the giant Matsushita Electrical Works, the president himself addresses the entire crew every morning in order to exhort them to greater efforts. Many Japanese companies look after their workers with what can only be termed as paternal benevolence by lending them money, giving them free medical care, and even arranging their marriages in some cases.

Thus Japanese workers are dedicated to their work and, taken collectively, are perhaps the hardest workers in the world. And when they work in unison they are capable of generating an extraordinary amount of energy and vitality. Such hustle and bustle a foreigner witnesses upon his

42

arrival in Tokyo is not seen anywhere else in the world. The sight of rush-hour commuters pushing and being shoved into inter-urban train coaches in Tokyo and elsewhere in Japan by platform attendants, is but one evidence of the tremendous vitality of which the Japanese are capable. Japanese energy is bursting at the seams. The sum total of the energy produced by 100 million Japanese by their antlike activities cannot be measured by the simple mathematical calculation of multiplying one's activity by 100 million. Rather the figure is multiplied by progressive and accelerated numbers which might run into the billions. It is as though when an atom is split it generates innumerable particles which in turn generate heat, there by producing energy which defies mere mathematics.

Japanese Abroad

IT IS A familiar sight nowadays to see a large number of Japanese tourists, often bespectacled and with a camera strapped on their shoulders, strolling along the main thoroughfares of the world's major cities. The Japanese are visiting Western countries in increasing numbers, either for business or on sightseeing tours. Japanese today, like Americans, are the world's greatest travelers, and to major airline companies of the world, Japanese are fast becoming the best customers. It is said that whenever an airliner crashes in any part of the world, which fortunately is a rare occurrence, there is always a Japanese passenger or two among the victims.

Since the restriction on foreign travel by Japanese was lifted in 1964 by the easing of foreign exchange controls, more and more Japanese are going abroad. It is common today for private schools to organize a group excursion of several weeks' duration to Europe and America for their students during the summer. It is also the practice now for affluent Japanese to spend New Year's in Hawaii or California. In all these cases the cost of travel is very high on account of the isolated geographical position of Japan, but the high cost evidently does not deter the Japanese from going abroad.

With most Japanese "going abroad" is almost a passion. In the early Meiji period soon after the country was opened to foreign intercourse, the Japanese started to go abroad in large numbers, and were most eager, as they are today, to visit Europe and America. Many Japanese go abroad on some specific mission, but many more do so merely to satisfy their curiosity. Many Japanese artists and scholars cherish a visit to Paris as their life-long ambition. "Don't die before you have seen Paris," they often say. The picture of chic Parisians lounging in a road-side cafe is so alluring and irresistible that a Japanese would, once in his lifetime, wish that he himself could be sitting and sipping coffee in a *bistro* on the Champs-Élysée.

Today since foreign travel has been made so easy (provided one has money), Japanese in all walks of life go abroad. Not long ago an influential public opinion survey agency in Japan conducted a poll among high school students as to which country they would like to visit most. The result was 75 per cent Switzerland, then came the United

States, England, France, and so on. To many Japanese Switzerland conjures up a picture of superb natural beauty and a happy and contented people. While nobody disputes such an image of Switzerland, the Japanese are ignorant of the fact that the scenery of their own land is just as superb, if not more beautiful and in fact more variegated than that of Switzerland. The pity of it all is that the Japanese are marring such superlative beauty, often by their hideous constructions and, unfortunately, with overcrowdedness.

Many Japanese also wish to go abroad merely to enhance their prestige and social standing. It is easy to exploit the naïveté and ignorance of their own people, concerning foreign countries. If a dressmaker says she is a graduate of a Paris fashion academy, for instance, she is sure to attract many customers. Such is the credulity and almost blind reverence of things Western among the Japanese. No one bothers to inquire or investigate whether the institute the dressmaker is said to have attended is a well-known one or how long she studied in Paris. The fact that she has been to Paris is enough to impress the unsuspecting customers.

Politicians, too, would not command much respect in their own electorate if they had never been abroad. So not only the leaders of major political parties but also assemblymen of provincial city councils, vie with one another in their junketing around the world. They usually vote a large sum of the local government budget as an extraordinary item to enable them to "study" the government system in America or Europe. The budget is easily approved as other assemblymen will sooner or later be following suit and be the potential beneficiaries. The taxpayers do not particularly protest such lavish and unwarranted expenditure as they are naïve enough not to suspect the assemblymen's ulterior motives.

Thus hundreds of thousands of Japanese every year find their way to Europe and America on one pretext or another in a constant stream. While such an exodus no doubt stimulates the progress of technology and accelerates Europeanization or Americanization of Japan which otherwise tends to remain isolated from the rest of the world, it is doubtful if any of these Japanese visitors really feel at home in America or Europe. For one thing, the massive stone or concrete buildings of the West not only impress the Japanese travelers but rather overwhelm them. True, Japanese cities abound with Western-style buildings which certainly are no novelties to the Japanese. But then European or American structures are by far the more massive and awe inspiring, with the result that the serene nerves of the average Japanese are unwittingly ruffled. In due course they begin to miss the light wooden structures and small landscape gardens to which they have so long been accustomed.

A veteran Japanese diplomat, who had served in a number of European capitals with distinction and who later became a foreign minister, once composed a poem while he was stationed at his last post in Europe. The poem was to the effect that though he was living in the glamor and luxury of diplomatic life, he would sooner go home and even longed to see a full moon through a torn paper screen of his wooden house back in Japan. The Japanese version of "Home, Sweet Home." This retreat to solitude or the desire to be close to nature, which borders on melancholic pessimism, is a very common trait with the Japanese which manifests itself more strongly as one ages.

In the matter of food, again, juicy, king-sized steaks are welcomed by a Japanese tourist for the first few days of his stay abroad. It is indeed a welcome change from the comparatively meager meat dishes he is used to at home. In no time, however, he begins to miss the light simple cooking of boiled rice, fish, and soybean sauce. If the trip lasts more than a month, the traveler becomes very unhappy and begins to show signs of irritation and nervousness as a result of eating non-Japanese food. The cure for such melancholia is to go to a Chinese or Japanese restaurant, if there is one. Most Chinese restaurants in the big cities of America or Europe are patronized by Japanese who relish Chinese dishes as a substitute for Japanese.

Japanese embassies and consulates overseas are invariably oases for Japanese travelers dying for their own native food. And it is unthinkable that a Japanese ambassador abroad would entertain an important visitor from home with a Western-style dinner. If he did he would become unpopular and might even be liable for demotion in due course. Incidentally, I have heard from many of my European colleagues that their own embassies nowadays are becoming four- or five-star restaurants for their VIP's from home.

Apart from these handicaps, Japanese suffer

from an inordinate sense of racial inferiority. Physically Japanese do not cut a very attractive figure and they are exceedingly self-conscious in the company of Occidentals. This accounts in part for the fact that Japanese tip so lavishly when they are abroad. By so doing they hope to curry the good will of hotel porters and others, thereby mitigating their sense of inferiority—fancied or real.

The Japanese are as human as any other people. Japanese travelers while abroad, naturally wish to sample a little bit of the night life of Western cities. Many of them, therefore, are tempted into nocturnal adventures with much curiosity and trepidation. However, Japanese tourists in the major cities of the world are known to obtain the favors of those mercenary devotees of Venus at a price generally twice that asked of other foreign clientele.

Thus, however much the Japanese may revel in the wonders of the West while traveling abroad, they eventually heave a sigh of relief when they get back to Haneda Airport. "Be it ever so humble, there's no place like home," the adage goes, but with the Japanese the proverb holds the greatest truth. Somehow the Japanese feel ill at ease in the West. This is one of the reasons why there are very few Japanese who settle permanently abroad. Chinese, as Orientals, enjoy no greater advantage physically or otherwise than Japanese. Yet the Chinese settle wherever there is a chance to make a decent living, even under adverse circumstances.

In the United States, apart from nisei, or the second-generation Japanese who consider the country as their own, very few Japanese have ever made good or settled there. In the thirties a certain Mr. Fujimura went to New York as an employee of the now defunct Asahi Silk Corporation. Silk then constituted a major Japanese export item to the United States. Fujimura, aside from his company's business, started speculating on the fluctuation of silk prices, and in due course made a fortune. In fact he was one of the most astute and enterprising Japanese businessmen that ever lived in the United States. He bought a large estate in Connecticut and lived a luxurious life with a Caucasian mistress. One winter he went on a cruise to Bermuda aboard one of the Atlantic luxury liners, and while en route mysteriously disappeared following an evening of heavy gambling. I happened to be a Japanese consul in the United States at the time and was instrumental in executing his will and remitting some of his fortune to his family back home. The money which his wife alone received ran into millions of dollars, and a dollar in those days could buy a good full-course dinner! Japanese like Fujimura are indeed few and far between.

Switzerland, as I wrote earlier, is considered a dreamland for many Japanese. The Lake of Geneva district abounds in villas and mansions of the world's millionaires. I know for a fact that not a few wealthy Chinese and Indians own property along the lake, but I know of not a single Japanese who ever cared to buy property there, let alone to settle down.

Since Japan was opened to the outside world some 100 years ago after centuries of self-imposed seclusion, some Japanese did immigrate, notably to California, British Columbia, and Brazil, where they first worked as contractual laborers or farmers and eventually settled down. Japanese, however, do not expatriate easily, and also because of racial discrimination, the total number of those Japanese immigrants may not exceed one million at most.

Japanese immigrants are generally hard working and regard work as a virtue rather than a necessary evil. Those of Japanese descent are successful through willingness to work as a family. In the United States, and in California in particular, Japanese are known to be excellent gardeners. In fact many American-born Japanese are engaged by wealthy Caucasians to tend their gardens on contractual bases. Japanese gardeners, silently and intensely, work from early morning till dusk— mowing lawns and tending flower gardens with painstaking care. This, like farming, is the line of occupation best suited to Japanese, inasmuch as the work involves little human contact or negotiation.

Though industrious, Japanese immigrants work largely on their own and seldom help each other in their communities abroad. On the contrary, there is a great deal of jealousy, rivalry, and petty recrimination among them. If one is successful in a certain field of business, others will soon come out to compete with him and even try to undermine his business. If, for example, a Japanese immigrant starts operating a Japanese restaurant and does well, in no time other Japanese will follow suit in the same district, with the end result that no one gets ahead due to cutthroat competition. This sorry phenomenon stems from the Japanese narrow, insular mentality and is in glaring contrast with overseas Chinese who make good wherever they may be by dint of mutual assistance and cooperation.

One of the reasons why Japanese are seriously hampered in their overseas expansion is their wretched command of foreign languages. The average Japanese may study English for years on end but somehow does not succeed in acquiring any fluency in speaking the language. Shortly after the last war there was a great enthusiasm for learning English among students and teachers, in spite of the fact that only certain private high schools had trained English teachers from abroad. Many teachers, who were long accustomed to the translation method of instruction, switched to the direct method which stressed oral training. Today, however, the improved method of teaching English, with emphasis on the oral approach, is slowly disappearing due to the pressure of preparing for entrance examinations which emphasize English grammar and composition. So, despite the fact that more and more Japanese are learning English —many out of sheer necessity—their achievements are not at all commensurate with the time and effort spent in the attempt. The Japanese simply do not seem to be endowed with a flair for languages.

Years ago an eminent Japanese publicist visited England, and was invited to address a group at a college in Cambridge on the Japanese political situation. Naturally the Japanese lecturer made a frantic effort to make his lecture a success, paying special attention to his English pronunciation. After the talk was over an Englishman in the audience remarked: "How very similar the Japanese language sounds to English."

Because of this language handicap Japanese immigrants seem to congregate largely in their own colony wherever they go, though the situation has much improved of late mainly because their children, the nisei, now speak the language of their adopted country. It is an astonishing fact that apart from immigrant farmers, 99 per cent of the Japanese who reside abroad, are dependent for their livelihood in some form or other on Japan. Young students, technicians, businessmen, newspapermen, Peace Corps workers in Asian countries—almost all usually get remittances from Japan. Few of them work their own way or are self-supporting. Even the operators of some of the Japanese restaurants in Europe receive subsidies from cultural organizations in Japan!

In recent years, however, Japanese businessmen are penetrating many parts of the world as representatives of big manufacturing industries. They are even setting up assembly plants in various parts of Europe and America in cooperation with local business interests. No doubt they are enterprising and can even be termed aggressive, but then they are acting collectively and are usually backed by their powerful parent organizations. As an individual a Japanese is forlorn and usually lacking in courage and in the spirit of enterprise. He is, when abroad, self-effacing and timid to the point of hypocrisy.

In prewar years a Japanese foreign exchange

53

bank of world-wide renown employed hundreds of Britons in its London offices. I can recall that whenever a Japanese member came from Japan to join the branch office, he was often referred to as a "student" by the British employees. Even today Japanese establishments abroad employing a European or American staff, seem to experience considerable difficulty in dealing with the foreign employees. Their labor relations ofttimes present a comic picture. In the first place, the Japanese normally pay inordinately high salaries to the Occidental employees in order to curry their favor and cooperation.

The Japanese will not call their foreign employees by their first names; they are afraid that would not be polite. Also the practice is not common in Japan. So a European driver or a messenger boy is often addressed as Mr. So-and-So by his Japanese employer. Japanese employers also find it difficult to admonish foreign staff members, which often results in the latter becoming overly familiar, if not out-right contemptuous. I have often witnessed Japanese employers requesting their foreign employees to "please" do this or that!

Japanese paternalism is very much in evidence in places where foreigners are employed. Once someone is employed the Japanese would not fire him summarily, even if his service is not satisfactory. In Japan most people make their employment a lifetime job and seldom quit. This practice makes up for the lack of social security measures. Likewise, in Japanese offices, European staff members are often retained for many years, perhaps because of Japanese leniency and also possibly because of generous wages, and by the fact that it is a time-honored practice of the Japanese to pay an extra month's pay for a year's service to each employee.

In one of the Japanese embassies in Europe a locally employed typist worked for 30 years. When she retired she was offered a free trip to Japan in recognition of her "meritorious" service. When the typist arrived in Tokyo, a big thanksgiving banquet was tendered in her honor, participated in by former ambassadors and an ex-foreign minister. For the rest of her sojourn in Japan, a VIP red-carpet treatment was meted out to her, much like the one accorded to visiting heads of state. Such acts of generosity are very common in labor relations where Japanese and Europeans are concerned.

Japanese are a gregarious people and as a group they are capable of displaying remarkable efficiency and ability. As an individual, on the other hand, a Japanese cuts a forlorn figure, especially when abroad. Nor is the Japanese a good mixer. Apart from his racial handicap the Japanese as a rule is a wretched linguist. Largely because of this linguistic difficulty, coupled with an innate shyness, most Japanese do not go out of their way to mix with Westerners. They find it a serious mental and physical strain to do so.

In these days of international conferences, Japanese take part in most major meetings. In particular, the United Nations is considered one of the most important fields of Japanese diplomacy. The Japanese press devotes considerable space to reporting activities of the United Nations and other international organizations. Ironically enough, despite the enormous importance attached to it, an international conference is the forum in which Japanese appear to be most feeble and unimpressive. Apart from language difficulties, the Japanese have neither the nerve nor audacity to speak out in public. They are meek, shy, and retiring. They betray considerable hesitation when called upon to intervene on the spur of the moment in a public debate. A Japanese is reserved by nature, and would rather keep quiet than to run the risk of making a laughing stock of himself by taking the floor without due preparation. A Japanese speaker at an international meeting almost always relies on a prepared manuscript. This fact, coupled with his usually inarticulate and low-pitched voice, makes the delivery often dull and uninspiring.

Chinese and Indians have produced not a few brilliant and extemporaneous speakers at international forums: Nehru, Wellington Koo, Krishna Menon, among others. Japan has yet to produce a speaker comparable to them. Lack of sense of humor with most Japanese is also responsible for this lamental state of affairs. I once presided over an annual general assembly of the International Labor Organization (ILO) in Geneva. When I was elected chairman many foreign delegates expressed misgivings as to whether I really was equal to the job; so rare was it a Japanese taking the chair of such a major international conference.

It is often said of a Japanese delegation to any conference that it is the 3–S delegation; the delegation characterized by Smile, Sleep, and Silence.

The Japanese smile when something is not particularly funny, or when they are not necessarily happy. They sometimes smile in order to gloss over an awkward situation. They also smile when they want to curry the favor of others. At an international conference they smile largely to make up for their silence and inactivities. The Japanese are also known to fall asleep, often at places where sleep is not warranted—in the trains and in their offices. While sleeping is normally considered a healthy sign—for so many people suffer from insomnia—the Japanese fall asleep mainly because of their heavy rice-eating and particularly because of their essentially happy-go-lucky nature. Thus the Japanese betray their own natural self so blatantly at international conferences in spite of themselves.

In postwar years one witnesses the proliferation of international organizations, from the United Nations in New York down to the United Nations Educational, Scientific and Cultural Organization (UNESCO) in Paris, the International Civil Aviation Organization (ICAO) in Montreal, the Food and Agriculture Organization (FAO) in Rome, the International Labor Organization (ILO) in Geneva, and so on. These international organizations, often better known by their abbreviations, maintain a secretariat staffed by cosmopolitan civil servants. Distribution of various posts in the secretariat is effected generally on the basis of the amount of contributions paid by member countries for the upkeep of the given organization. It is a remarkable fact that the Japanese employed in these agencies are few and far between, despite the fact that Japan today is one of the major contributors to the upkeep of those manifold international offices. The reasons for this anomaly are not too difficult to realize. One reason is that Japan, after the defeat in the last war, came back too late to join these organizations. Hence she was too late to scramble for various posts allocated on a national basis. The main reason, however, appears to be reluctance of the Japanese to work as international civil servants.

Apart from the language difficulty, the Japanese usually find the work in such cosmopolitan groups a severe mental strain. A reticent and self-effacing Japanese official will soon be outwitted, ignored, and finally demoted by his more aggressive foreign colleagues, and ends up leaving the organization in utter despair to seek more congenial employment among his own compatriots back home. If he is retained, he is usually given a quiet job which requires no great personal contact, such as a post in the research division. As a matter of fact, in the United Nations secretariat and other similar organizations, quite a few Japanese officials work in the statistical sections.

The Japanese, by and large, are shy and self-effacing people. They do not cut a brilliant figure in the international field mainly because of their innate insularity. It will indeed be many years before they can become more cosmopolitan, both in outlook and behavior.

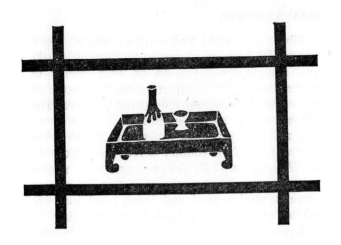

A Paradise for Foreigners

JAPAN, from a Westerner's point of view, cannot necessarily be a desirable place to live. For Europeans, in particular, despite rapidly shrinking distances in this jet age, Japan still continues to be a part of the Far East, and life in Japan with most long-time residents tends to be that of an exile.

Then there is the constant irritation of Oriental delays and procrastinations; of exaggerated politeness and overcrowded surroundings, to which some foreigners never seem to adjust. They keep on grumbling all the time and say how true Kipling was when he said: " ... and never the twain shall meet." Moreover, in recent years the high cost of living in Tokyo and elsewhere throughout the nation has become a factor which discourages foreign diplomats and businessmen from being stationed in Japan.

However, several tens of thousands of Europeans and Americans, mostly missionaries, teachers, and businessmen, do or even prefer to make their living in Japan primarily because of the comparatively easy life obtainable there. The climate, excepting the summer when it is damp and suffocating, is mild. In fact the climate in the central part of the country is very much like that of Washington, D.C. The most erroneous notion a Westerner gets about Japan is that the climate there is semi-tropical and living conditions are similar to those throughout Southeast Asia.

Japanese kindness and friendliness are also important factors in inducing some foreigners to stay in Japan. Japanese tolerance and the extraordinary regard in which the Japanese hold foreigners often prompt Westerners to make a living in Japan, especially when they have little prospect of a successful career in their own country. A few years ago an allegation was made in one of Tokyo's English-language dailies that not a few Occidentals who chose to live in Japan did so because they were homosexuals. Police are extremely lenient with foreigners, particularly Caucasians, and the foreigners could indulge in the practice with impunity, according to this rather sensational revelation.

Doctor Thomas Baty, a British authority on international law, was for many years legal advisor to the Japanese Foreign Ministry in prewar years. He was liberally paid and lived in an imposing Western-style house much like an embassy residence, rent free. When World War II broke out, Baty, a confirmed bachelor, refused to be repatriated, so enamored was he with the people who had been so kind and generous to him. Having ignored the advice of the local British Embassy to quit Japan, Baty was later declared a traitor by the British government. During the difficult war years, a certain Japanese banker placed his seaside villa at Dr. Baty's disposal, where he lived with ease and comfort for the rest of his life. When Baty died the Japanese government buried him in one of the best cemeteries in Tokyo with due pomp, and each year on the anniversary of his death commemorative services are held by his old friends even to this day.

Japanese universities and high schools used to employ, as they do now, English language instructors of European or American extraction on a contractual basis. In the high school that I attended there was a Scot who taught not only in my school but in several others in the district, as well. His wife, herself a Scot, was most enterprising and taught not only English but also gave piano lessons to the children of wealthy families. Being in Japan at the time when Britannia still ruled the seven seas and in a locality where foreigners were rarities meant a lot to him and his wife. Many well-to-do families in the city vied with one another to request the honor of the presence of this "English gentleman" and his "lady" at wedding receptions and other major social gatherings. Though undoubtedly a life of exile, this Scotch couple must have lived a life of extreme ease and of pecuniary advantage, much like British colonial officials of those days.

Years later when I was working in the London

Embassy, I was surprised to receive a telephone call one day from none other than this former English teacher. He and his wife had just arrived from Japan by boat and were in trouble. When I inquired as to the nature of their trouble they told me that they had brought back with them some 80 big wooden crates full of Japanese curios and other valuable articles on which the customs insisted that duties be paid. These items were all gifts from their former pupils and friends in Japan, and they wanted me to certify to the customs to that effect.

Japanese are inveterate gift-givers. The custom is widespread not only among themselves but is also employed when dealing with foreigners. A Japanese cannot, as a rule, call on his friend without taking some sort of gift—usually a box of cakes. When a Japanese dignitary goes abroad on an official mission, he usually takes pearl necklaces, transistor radios, or expensive silk fabrics as souvenirs and, almost like a Santa Claus, distributes these items to whomever he is to call upon. It is also a fairly common practice in Japan to distribute gifts to the guests at a cocktail party or wedding reception. A long-time foreign resident in Tokyo, a lawyer of rather unsavory reputation, is so used to the practice that he now exacts a present or two from any Japanese who visits his office as a preliminary to the business talk.

The Japanese are also great music lovers, and this applies more particularly to Western music. It is almost incredible that Japanese, who often find it difficult to discard their own traditional traits, should take to Western music so readily and with such gusto. In fact it is now more common to hear Western music in Tokyo or Osaka than it is to hear traditional Japanese music. Not only do Japanese love to listen to Western music but they themselves have produced not a few talents in the Western music field. There are as many as six symphony orchestras in Japan today. In recent years Japanese musicians have distinguished themselves in various international competitions, and it is not uncommon for a Japanese to conduct a Western orchestra as guest conductor. Because of this insatiable appetite for Western music, Tokyo is today fast becoming a mecca for many Occidental musicians of any note.

There was a time immediately after the war when Japanese, dying for Western music, would invite almost any Western musician on terms so attractive that the performer could make a small fortune from his tour of Japan. Even by paying the performers lavishly, promoters could still make good profits, so avid is the Japanese taste for Western music and so huge is the potential audience. A Japanese college student who has to make both ends meet on a budget of say 50 dollars a month, does not think anything about spending 10 dollars to attend a piano recital. Even today terms offered to Occidental musicians of note are said to far exceed those usually offered them for their appearance in New York. Though the Japanese are becoming more discriminating, Japan still continues to be a paradise for Occidental musicians.

The Japanese, perhaps because they are themselves poor linguists or probably because of their insularity, are deeply impressed when foreigners speak Japanese. Their admiration is all the greater if a foreigner speaks the language with any fluency. That a foreigner should speak the language of any country is considered a great compliment to the country. In Poland where I resided for some years, I learned Polish and spoke it with some fluency. The Poles were greatly flattered and would go out of their way to help me, and their kindness was overwhelming. Poles as a whole are an exceedingly kindhearted people, but I suspected that they found in me a friend who took pains to learn their own language, which incidentally is one of the most difficult in the world.

To a greater extent the Japanese appreciate those foreigners who speak Japanese. Their appreciation is mingled with admiration, which often borders on trust and confidence. Imitation is the best form of flattery, but to the average Japanese a Japanese-speaking foreigner is often looked upon as invariably pro-Japanese. If the foreigner's mastery of the language is complete, Japanese are often disarmed and feel quite at ease in the company of the foreigner. A resident Caucasian, if he or she speaks perfect Japanese, is very much in demand as a public relations man on television by commercial firms. The audience is impressed by the performance of such a person and warmly applauds. It goes without saying that these Japanese-speaking Caucasians are handsomely paid for their services.

Recently, English has been taught very extensively in Japan, both at schools and privately.

There are not a few Japanese, notably nisei, or American-born Japanese, who can speak perfect English and they themselves make good teachers. However, the Japanese employ American, Canadian, or British teachers of Caucasian origin in preference to nisei even though the schools have to pay a good deal more for the Europeans or Americans. An English language institute would not get enough pupils otherwise; so great is Japanese admiration of Westerners! I have known not a few cases of resident foreigners who exploited this Japanese weakness and waxed fat on their ill-gotten gains. This applies not only to Caucasians but also to foreigners from Asiatic countries.

Many Asians from neighboring countries who reside in Japan are by far the better linguists than the Japanese. In many cases a few years' residence in the country suffices to enable them to master the language. Some of them, because of their physical appearance, coupled with their linguistic proficiency, can behave almost like Japanese and seem to suffer from no great disadvantage. Moreover, many of these Asians, unlike Japanese, are generally endowed with business acumen and not a few are now known to be multi-millionaires. There is a belief among the Japanese that many of these Asian residents are unscrupulous in their business dealings, and that the Japanese are often victimized. This was probably the case during the immediate postwar years when these Asians enjoyed certain extraterritorial privileges in Japan under the Allied occupation. What advantages they enjoyed have now been largely liquidated, and today those foreign residents from neighboring countries are not in a particularly favorable position, legally or otherwise, save perhaps their easy mastery of the Japanese language which undoubtedly helps them in their dealings with the Japanese.

The Japanese are extremely lax in the matter of contracts. In fact, signing a written contract is essentially a Western practice, though in recent years many contracts are signed in Japan on international business deals. Oddly enough, few Japanese seem to grasp the importance of the signing of a contract. Many Japanese are seen signing papers without carefully going through the contents. They consider the signing more as a formality and tend to overlook how binding the terms of contracts can be. While the Japanese are cautious in dealing with their own folk, they easily fall into pitfalls when the other party happens to be a foreigner.

I have, during my services abroad, naturally had various Japanese assistants who worked under me. In particular those junior clerks who served abroad for the first time often caused me and my government irreparable financial losses. One young clerk once ordered the walls of an office room painted without first asking for the estimates from the contractor. When the work was finished we were presented with a bill ten times the normal painting cost. There was however, no crying over spilt milk. This young assistant learned a lesson at a high cost. Another time the office dismissed a dishonest driver, who later came back with a lawyer with a claim for a fabulous sum of money alleging an unjustified dismissal. I found out that this Japanese clerk, when last settling the money due to the driver, failed to obtain a statement that the driver had no further claim.

In Warsaw a Japanese friend of mine once took a Polish friend to a Jewish restaurant. When seated in the restaurant the Japanese host asked his Polish friend to order what the latter liked and what he thought was appropriate, since the the Japanese was not familiar with a Jewish menu. When the feasting was over the Japanese was presented with the bill, the amount of which was staggering. When he went home that evening he had a long argument with his wife who maintained that the cost of the evening represented a whole month's household expenses. His chagrin was so great that he could not sleep at all that night.

Thus the Japanese are known in Europe and elsewhere as easy prey to unscrupulous merchants and ruthless operators. The idea of right and obligation as understood in the West has but slightly entered into the minds of the Japanese. In Japan one may order a wall painted without first asking for the cost, but one is seldom charged more than what is usual. In some cases, particularly at a first-class Japanese restaurant, it is even considered impolite to ask for the charge before the service is rendered. A man who does so is often branded as ill-bred.

The Japanese by nature are not rapacious. Their own native land has provided essentially what they needed for their living for centuries. They have been accustomed from time immemorial to a frugal life and their want is generally modest. The Japanese have, in their long history, not suffered much from predatory attacks from neighboring countries, nor have they often embarked on similar expeditions themselves. Having been cut off from the rest of the world by surrounding seas, the Japanese tend to look upon foreigners as novelties and often as welcome guests. "Great is the joy to see a friend who comes from afar," is an old Oriental saying.

Several years ago a Danish sailor who stopped at a Japanese port was said to have been robbed of his belongings and valuables in a hotel room where he stayed. He reported his plight to the police, and next day newspapers carried the news of the alleged theft. Within a matter of days donations poured in from many unknown Japanese who wanted to help this hapless Dane. Cash donations alone amounted to some 200,000 yen, and the Danish sailor went home a rich man. The Japanese thinking is that since the Dane was a sort of guest in Japan, the fact that he should have been subject to a robbery was a disgrace to Japan. Hence it was for the Japanese to make amends.

Spying has been and still is a potent weapon in the hands of many governments. In time of war, belligerents as well as neutrals vie with one another to obtain military information of all kinds. Richard Sorge, a German spy who operated in Japan during the war, has since been brought to light as having been a double spy who also spied for the Soviet Union. In time of peace, too, spies of different kinds roam about in Japan and elsewhere. But nowhere is spying so easy as in the Japan of today. Legislations guarding state secrets were done away with after the war. Also, spying is made much easier by the very fact that a Japanese, when approached by a Westerner in a friendly way, is readily disarmed and will talk about anything without scruples.

There are also many "industrial spies" who come to Japan nowadays to fish for information on a sophisticated product or a highly efficient machine. From these latter-day spies on down to foreign diplomats, they find Japan a veritable paradise for their nefarious activities. As a matter of fact one East European ambassador stationed in Tokyo, recently told me that he did not experience any difficulty in collecting information in Japan. Just because there is no barrier to transmitting any news, information of a confidential nature is leaked to the Japanese press. Also the Japanese are very lax in the matter of guarding secrets, presumably because of their weak character as an individual. Today discussions which take place on highly sensitive subjects in the Foreign Ministry, for instance, often find their way into Japanese newspapers. Diligent perusal of Japanese newspapers and periodicals, then, suffices to get a fairly accurate picture of what is going on behind the scenes in Japan.

Many foreigners are known to have become rich by taking advantage of Japanese leniency and diffidence toward Caucasians. Prior to the Second World War there was an exodus of Jewish people from Europe due to the persecution initiated by Hitler. Tens of thousands of these refugees, often penniless, traveled by the trans-Siberian railway to Japan and from there on to the Americas. Japanese trans-Pacific steamship companies enjoyed a good business in this wholesale migration of Jews from Europe.

A Jewish woman who traveled steerage class on a N.Y.K. ship from Yokohama to Vancouver in 1939, eventually became a millionaire by what was believed by everyone to be a ruse. One stormy day while she was walking on the promenade deck, she claimed that she had tripped over a spittoon placed in a corner of the deck. The woman maintained that she was badly shaken by the accident, and later developed a serious mental disorder. Upon landing at Seattle she engaged a Jewish lawyer and sued the N.Y.K. for negligence in placing the spittoon in an inappropriate place. Not only the shipping company but also fellow passengers who witnessed the alleged accident, knew full well that it was more a theatrical act than anything else. The N.Y.K. manager in Seattle at the time told me that, however flimsy the plaintiff's case might have been, there was little chance of the company defending itself inasmuch as the woman seemed to be working closely with her lawyer and court officials. Thereupon the company easily gave in and settled the case by paying her 10,000 dollars as a solatium, which 30 years ago represented perhaps ten times the present value of the dollar. With this money as capital, this enterprising Jewish woman started a business in the United States. Together with her son she is today known to be a millionaire.

For many years Japan has floated bonds both in London and New York to finance her industrial programs. Considerable foreign currency loans were also contracted for soon after the great earthquake disaster of 1923. Japan was an unknown country in those early years and was naturally considered as an investment risk. The first sterling loan ever floated in England, which was to finance the construction of the first railway line in Japan— between Tokyo and Yokohama in 1870—carried an unheard of interest rate of nine per cent per annum. Even today Japan usually has to abide by somewhat disadvantageous terms when trying to float an external loan, and a Japanese government bond traded in the world financial centers is quoted rather cheaply when compared with those of other governments, presumably because foreign investors even today are not quite convinced of Japan's credit worthiness.

Be that as it may, Japan has a very proud record of having scrupulously carried out foreign bond obligations during the last 100 years. During the Second World War, however, Japan had to suspend temporarily the servicing of both sterling and dollar bonds, the total amount of which ran into billions of dollars. In 1952 when the peace treaty was signed, foreign bondholders' associations, both in London and New York, started negotiations with the Japanese government with a view to securing resumption of the debt service. Similar negotiations were also carried out at the time between Germany, another defeated and impoverished country, and the Anglo-Saxon groups. Germany maintained all along that she could ill afford to continue to pay the high interest rates paid on her prewar Dawes and Young loans now that the country was reduced to near financial insolvency. The Germans thus bargained with the

British and Americans and finally succeeded in obtaining a reduction in the interest rate when they agreed to resume the servicing of the bonds contracted for in prewar years.

The Japanese negotiators, on the other hand, never grumbled about their difficulty in meeting Japan's debt, let alone ask for reduction in interest payments. They agreed unilaterally to all the conditions proposed by the Anglo-American bondholders. Japan not only consented to continue to pay the high interests rates stipulated on prewar loans but also ungrudgingly took upon herself the obligation of those bonds issued by various ex-Japanese colonial enterprises in Korea, Manchuria, and Formosa, whose assets had been confiscated by the succeeding governments established there after the war. It is universally recognized by international law that those succeeding governments should be held responsible for the assets as well as liabilities of the enterprises which were taken over by the incoming governments.

It is not hard to see that in the debt settlement of 1952, Japan was motivated by a sincere desire to uphold her excellent credit standing, believing that such magnanimous concessions made on the prewar debt settlement would pay handsomely in the future. Yet in contrast to the Germans, who were placed in a similar position, the Japanese did not so much as try to bargain or negotiate; an astounding fact which merely demonstrated the good naturedness of the Japanese.

While Japan has a highly developed taxation system with emphasis on direct taxation, tax collection is not always strictly enforced vis-a-vis foreigners. Also entries in tax declaration forms are so cumbersome that even well-meaning foreign residents often fail to comply with the procedures. The result is that while big foreign corporations operating in Japan may be paying taxes as stipulated and apart from those whose revenues are deducted at source, individual foreigners often evade tax payment and are not penalized thereby.

There are also legal loopholes and omissions of various kinds in the system itself, and the Japanese tax bureau is relatively lenient with respect to foreigners. In fact Japanese tax laws have been compared to a kimono that "covers all, touches nothing." A foreigner visiting the United States, even for a short visit, has to report to an Interior Revenue office before he finally leaves the country to make sure that he has paid the stipulated income and other taxes. No such control is in force in Japan, with the result that a foreigner can leave the country scot free after having closed a deal which is legally taxable. Japanese leniency toward foreigners is manifested in many ways, but in the field of taxation the government seems to be particularly lax and ineffective.

The Japanese government, like other governments, is rather hesitant about foreign banking corporations opening branches in Japan. For a foreign bank it is not always easy to get a license to operate in Japan, except on a basis of reciprocity. But once the license is granted the Japanese Finance Ministry is surprisingly lenient toward the foreign bank. Banks operating in Japan, both foreign and domestic, are by regulations subject to periodic inspection of their books by government authorities. It is a surprising fact, therefore, that branches of foreign banking corporations in Japan have been almost free from such inspections; there have been only two instances of foreign bank inspection since 1945. On the other hand Japanese banks are constantly being inspected and their officers interrogated by Bank of Japan and Finance Ministry officials. Apparently Japanese inspectors are reluctant to visit foreign banks mainly because they feel vaguely awed by Westerners, and some, are even overtly afraid of foreigners.

There have in recent years been many joint ventures set up by Japanese and foreign interests which are operating in Japan. In such companies the Japanese retain a slightly higher than 50 per cent capitalization for obvious reasons. In some cases board meetings are conducted in English, with the result that Japanese directors, usually unable to speak the language well, are at the mercy of non-Japanese directors who can impose their will freely upon their Japanese counterparts. A joint company is a Japanese company incorporated in Japan in accordance with the Corporation Law of Japan and therefore must conform to the Japanese rules and regulations. Japanese directors, however, by allowing board meetings to be conducted in English, are placing themselves in a disadvantageous position. In many instances a joint enterprise, once set up in Japan, in no time finds itself dominated by minority foreign interests.

This is in glaring contrast to some of the Asian countries which resort to drastic measures of nationalizing foreign property without any compensation. True, there have been times in the recent history of Japan since the country was opened to foreign intercourse, when foreigners were subject to abuse and humiliation. Waves of xenophobia have swept the country from time to time; particularly was it the case during the years immediately prior to the Pacific War. Many Westerners were looked upon as spies, and their movements were closely watched by members of a special secret police. Some were even apprehended and put into prison.

It is a remarkable fact that even at the height of such anti-foreignism, the Japanese at heart were kind and helpful to the Westerners. When World War II finally broke out in 1941, and the resident British and Americans were herded into protective custody at various camps as enemy aliens, many Japanese sneaked into the camps at night and presented their enemy friends with delicacies and other food items which the Japanese themselves could ill afford.

In fact what anti-foreignism that might have existed in the minds of Japanese throughout their history, is a reflection largely of the inferiority complex from which the Japanese invariably suffer toward Westerners and Western civilization. At heart the Japanese have always admired, and even secretly revered Westerners and things Western. Occasional outbursts of xenophobia, then, are the other face of the coin, so to speak; the other face being profound reverence in which the Occidentals are held in the mind of the Japanese.

The Japanese, in their understandable desire to have the country better known to the outside world, go to great lengths to invite all kinds of foreigners to Japan. Most other countries nowadays also undertake such public relations work; from mutual exchange visits of high government dignitaries to granting scholarships to students. Japanese invitations, however, are much more extensive and generous.

In many cases a foreigner of any note, be he a statesman, scientist, or businessman, gets an invitation to visit Japan by government or other agencies, often with all expenses borne by the host. The visitor during his stay, is royally entertained, provided with a guide or interpreter wherever he goes, and is given a souvenir gift or two which is often quite expensive. In recent years the Japanese have coined the term "invitational diplomacy," which in effect means that those free trips offered to foreign VIP's constitute an important part of Japanese diplomatic activities.

The Olympic Games held in Tokyo in 1964 may also be cited as an example of this Japanese anxiety to have the country better known abroad. The zeal with which the Japanese had prepared for the Games was almost pathetic. Before the vote was taken by the International Olympic Committee for Tokyo as the venue for the 1964 Games, the Japanese government must have spent millions of dollars by inviting Olympic officials of various countries to come to Japan to see the facilities available, and also by dispatching numerous Japanese delegations and individuals to canvass for the Olympics. When objection was raised by smaller and distant countries against

Tokyo on account of the distance and expenses involved, the Japanese authorities even offered to bear some of the expenses. No sooner the Olympic Games were over than Japan embarked on another prestige project—the holding of a world fair at Osaka in 1970. To the Japanese cost is no serious consideration. They would sacrifice anything to achieve their supreme objective; namely, to enhance the prestige of Japan in the eyes of the world.

A similar motive has prompted the Japanese government to play host to major international organizations, such as the International Atomic Energy Agency (IAEA), the General Agreement on Tariffs and Trade (GATT), and others. These agencies have their own secretariat in Europe and normally do not rotate their annual convention among the different capitals of member countries. To hold a general assembly away from the seat of the secretariat naturally entails staggering sums of money. Not only the delegates but the secretariat staff, including stenographers and interpreters, had to travel all the way to Tokyo with their files and documents. Yet the Japanese government very generously offered to bear all the extra expense, including per diem for hundreds of the secretariat staff not only during the conference but also while they were en route to and from Japan. And, those who attended the Tokyo meetings were given suitable presents. No other government has offered to play host to these international agencies on such lavish, often humiliating terms.

However, the Japanese people derive tremendous satisfaction and pride from such acts of generosity, and the sacrifices and expenses thereby incurred seem amply compensated for by the fact that an international agency of any importance has held its major session in Tokyo. Such self-satisfaction is due, in my view, to an inordinate sense of inferiority from which the average Japanese suffer toward Westerners. This was particularly the case during the postwar period which followed the American occupation of the country. At the same time, unbounded Japanese hospitality bordering on absurdity, coupled with an innate sense of insularity, are also responsible for these extraordinary efforts to induce foreigners to come to Japan.

Metropolis to Megalopolis

THE FIRST glimpse of Japan is apt to be disappointing to the visitor; the environs of Haneda Airport and the Yokohama and Kobe dock areas are definitely less picturesque or colorful than are most national entrance gateways. The first impression of Tokyo is one of overwhelming ugliness and unbelievable congestion. I have known not a few Western diplomats who, upon arriving in Tokyo for the first time, were so disappointed that they decided then and there to quit the country after a minimum tenure of service.

Driving into Tokyo on an elevated express highway, one is struck with a glaring contrast presented by a huge conglomeration of flimsy, native wooden houses down below and massive steel and concrete super highways. In endlessly

79

monotonous vistas, unimpressive buildings crouch under a sky scarred by a grid of overhead cables. By comparison with most European and American cities, Japanese cities are dusty, drab, over-populated, and lacking in elementary facilities. The country's roads, though greatly improved in recent years, are, for the most part, still narrow and badly surfaced.

Tokyo is without any really great avenues; it has nothing to compare with New York's Park Avenue and certainly nothing to compare with Paris' boulevards. Due to an inexorable growth in motor traffic, some streets have in recent years been widened at a staggering cost—the cost largely accounting for the sequestration of precious little privately owned grounds—and some freeways and express highways have been constructed. These motor arteries are, however, due chiefly to limitation in space, a far cry from American and European counterparts, being generally narrow and undistinguished in appearance.

Hardly anything old and historic is left standing, and the Palace moat and walls are perhaps the only major reminder that the city dates back to Edo, three centuries ago. Tokyo's parks are a shambles, and its open spaces and gardens are so shabby that they would not be tolerated in other capitals. Hibiya Park, the central park of Tokyo, for instance, is so small that it can hardly be called a park in the Western sense of the word. Flower beds and fountains which dot the park, are often unartistic, while trees and shrubs are seedy and unkempt.

Japanese, from olden days, used to frequent

temples and shrines, not only for worship but for recreation as well. Temple and shrine precincts, then, have played the role of public parks in Japan in days gone by. In fact some of the shrine compounds are pleasant, spacious, and even impressive. Meiji Shrine in Tokyo, which enshrines Emperor Meiji who reigned from 1868 to 1912, has a garden which is a delight to strollers. The Grand Shrine of Ise in central Japan which is dedicated to the sun goddess, the legendary founder of the Japanese Empire, has a compound so spacious and so impressive that it attracts visitors from all over the country.

Parks built in larger cities, on the other hand, are essentially an imported institution and as such the Japanese are not always capable of landscaping them in the way they should be. Japanese are not very good at building foreign-style edifices, any more so than are Westerners capable of constructing typically Japanese creations. If, for instance, a foreigner tries to build a Japanese-style house, the result often turns out to be a monstrosity in the eyes of the Japanese. Similarly, the Japanese, when they attempt a Western-style public park, are not particularly successful. Thus despite the high standards of contemporary Japanese architects, only a handful of the new buildings in Tokyo are of any distinction. Most big ferro-concrete buildings, while thoroughly modern in design and concept, somehow lack in elegance or are out of proportion, for the reason I have just mentioned with respect to the parks.

Sumida River, the Hudson River of Tokyo, is fast becoming polluted with waste of all kinds and is nothing anymore but a huge gutter. The riverside is drab and dingy and has been devoted to industry, commercial uses, the poorer classes of residences, and at best, seedy parks. Certainly there is nothing in Tokyo to compare with the riverside development of the Thames, the Hudson, or the Seine.

Away from the city center, streets are narrow and dirty, lined with rickety houses with open-fronted booths gaudily embellished with neon lights and signs. The percentage of road space against total area is only half that of major American cities. Yet there are already over a million motor vehicles in operation. Only about 20 per cent of Tokyo homes are connected with the municipal sewage system; and even if the rest were, there would not be enough water to serve them.

Thus Tokyo, of all Japanese cities, is almost an unplanned, haphazardly overgrown urban area, unworthy of the name of a capital city. Kyoto, which was the capital of Japan before Tokyo, like its predecessor Nara, is a better-planned city, symmetrically laid out with a certain amount of zoning already enforced as far back as the 10th century. Tokyo has had the misfortune of having been almost totally destroyed twice in the last half century—first in the great earthquake-fire of 1923 in which 150,000 people perished, and again during World War II by a series of incendiary bombings. On both occasions city fathers missed a unique chance of reconstructing the metropolis on a more permanent basis. Instead, in the wake of each of these two catastrophies, reconstruction was left more or less to take care of itself and no farsighted planning was ever instituted.

So Tokyo, proud of being the largest city in the world, population wise, remains basically a conglomeration of villages. It sprawls endlessly around urban centers, with a tousled network of badly paved, ill-lit streets and country lanes—a teeming monster of metropolitan growth, and the despair of town planners and civic administrators.

Perhaps the most impressive sight of Tokyo is at night as when viewed from the air. The whole of Tokyo is a vast sparkle of light with occasional thicker concentrations of luminosity which appear to be amusement centers such as Ueno, Shibuya, and the Ginza. The lamps of side streets in comparatively darker areas are pale golden chains, touched with searing jewels of neon—great white stacks of fevered brilliance—heartlessly clear and vivid; remote dots of light on a dusky dark ground. This vast sea of billions of fairy lights extends for miles on end and presents a nocturnal panorama not reproduced in any other world capital. For unlike Western cities, Tokyo streets remain brilliantly lit all through the night, and many open-fronted shops and flimsily built houses from which light seeps out into the streets, add an extraordinary brilliance which only a city the size of Tokyo can produce.

Tokyo's population was reduced to three million at the end of World War II, but has grown to 11 million today on much the same land area. Per capita, space for Tokyo is a mere 0.4 square meter, compared with Paris' 8.7, London's 9.2, New York's 11.9, and Washington's 45.2. Overcrowding is aggravated by poor sanitation and a perennial water shortage, while the municipal fire brigades cannot hope to cope with the numerous fires, big and small, that break out in dry winter months throughout the city. The activities of fire fighters are always hampered by the low pressure of water mains and also by narrow streets which make access to the scene of the fire supremely difficult.

Sheer size of the population renders garbage collection an almost impossible task. Garbage-collecting vehicles that periodically circulate in the city, are so tiny that they are far too inadequate to cope with the huge amounts of waste which accumulate as householders place their garbage on their front door steps in expectation of the vehicle's visit. Often the garbage containers and extra cardboard boxes full of refuse remain heaped together in front of homes for days on end, when the collectors fail to come around on appointed days. Disposal of the collected garbage also leaves much to be desired; there being no large-scale incinerators nor enough dumping grounds for the voluminous waste and refuse produced daily by 11 million inhabitants.

Speaking of garbage, Tokyo parks and playgrounds are often littered in the wake of a picnic by school children or a garden party, or by a mass demonstration. Participants in such outings nonchalantly throw away empty lunch boxes, waste paper, orange peels, and indeed almost anything for which they have no further use. Most Japanese do not bother to take such refuse away or dispose of it themselves. Besides, what waste paper baskets or dustbins provided in public places are so few and usually so small that they are far too inadequate to cope with the demand.

On a long-distance train in Japan it is the same story. Passengers dump empty lunch boxes, bottles and cans, cigarette butts and ashes, indiscriminately all over the floor. Every few hours a gang of sweepers comes around to clean up the aisle from one end to the other, but in no time the coach floor again becomes littered with refuse.

Japanese are reputed to be a clean people; their habit of taking a daily bath, constant sweeping and dusting of their house, keeping the floor immaculately clean—these are some of the features of Japanese cleanliness. But this cleanliness stops abruptly on the threshold of their own home or at the confines of their immediate environment. There is a popular saying in Japan: "One is free from shame while on a trip," meaning that one is scot free to behave in whatever manner he pleases once he goes on a trip. There is in fact no better description of Japanese behavior in public places than this time-honored saying.

A Japanese has been subject from time immemorial to all sorts of regimentations, both mental and otherwise, within his own family circle or his community. For example, a young child is taught to behave inobtrusively in the presence of others and to be always polite to his elders. A young girl is also told to behave gently on all occasions for fear that "others may laugh at you," or if she is married, to do her utmost to please her fastidious "in-laws." In prewar days a young girl even had to learn to sleep straight, with her legs together. Thus the Japanese are placed under constant mental restraint while at home in order to conform to prescribed etiquette and behavior. So once outside the confines of his home or family, a Japanese is at last "liberated" from all these restraints and starts behaving like a different person.

For instance, a Japanese soldier sent to Southeast Asia during the war was capable of committing unbelievable atrocities, for he was "shame free" outside his own home or country. And so it is that if a street is littered or a public park is in a disgraceful state, the average Japanese does not give a hoot. The degree of selfishness, rudeness, and inconsideration shown in public conveyances in Japan also cannot be surpassed. Such antisocial behavior of the Japanese can only be properly understood in the context I have just explained.

It must be mentioned in fairness to my compatriots, however, that the streets of Western cities, too, are often not clean or tidy. A walk along New York's Broadway on Saturday night is enough to let one know how hopelessly littered that famous thoroughfare is. I have also seen a street in London which is not only littered with trash but is also covered all over the place with animal waste. In some Western cities, however, streets are cleaned more regularly and systematically by machines, but these cities are not half as crowded as Japanese cities, and litter is that much less and the cleaning is thus made that much easier. And, Western streets being wider, are easier to clean.

As for the enormous amount of garbage dumped on a park lawn or in the aisle of a train coach, there is no excuse. Japanese are a wasteful people—wasteful in the sense that most things like chopsticks and lunch containers are discarded after one use. Also the Japanese use enormous amounts of paper for wrapping, as is evidenced when shopping in a big department store. Any article bought is always wrapped by a shop girl. When giving a gift to some one the item is always wrapped in beautiful paper, for, according to Japanese etiquette it is not proper to advertise what is being presented. It may embarrass both the giver and the recipient if the item happens to be of no great value. The recipient, too, when he receives the gift, does not open the box or package to see what the gift is, let alone to admire it on the spot. This is another example of Japanese modesty, timidity, and above all, the aversion to ostentation.

Despite the fact that the city is already overcrowded, the influx of people to Tokyo continues unabated. During the past five years, people have been moving into the capital at a rate of 220,000 a year—that is, every year a population the size of Geneva is being added to the already overcrowded city, making the problems of housing, transportation, and water supply even more difficult.

The main attraction appears to be the higher living standards offered by the capital city, where two-thirds of the major business firms of the nation are concentrated, as well as one-third of the institutions of cultural and higher learning, and the government with all its ministries. Some of the Western-style hotels in Tokyo are luxurious and well appointed and compare favorably with any of the first-class hotels in the West. One can also find restaurants of different national tastes, not only Japanese and Western but also Indian, Persian, Russian, and even Jewish.

Almost anything salable in London or New York is sold in Tokyo. French cosmetics and perfumes, American bowling equipment and limousines, private aircraft, modern paintings, and antique furniture—all find takers at fat prices. For in Tokyo wealth is concentrated as never before, and with an influx of foreigners for business and sightseeing it is fast becoming a cosmopolitan city. Tokyo has an insatiable market, and consumer demands keep growing. There are over 150,000 shops and stores employing a million people—almost one tenth of the population. Tokyo earns over 22 per cent of the national income. Big business is getting bigger and many a man who was formerly a modest farmer on the city's outskirts, is now a multimillionaire. In the past decade, Tokyo land prices have increased at an average rate of nearly 20 per cent per year.

The population has spread out over the Kanto plain like prairie fire; yet the congestion is unrelieved. Renovation and relocation projects are being undertaken, but the snowballing growth of the population has created a tremendous strain on the city's housing and other facilities. In order to reverse the influx, various proposals such as the deconcentration of offices and their dispersal to satellite towns are much discussed, but apparently without any tangible results. For in Japan there is a great gap in living standards and amenities offered by Tokyo and provincial cities; the disparity being such that once someone has lived in Tokyo for any length of time, it would be hard for him to go back to live in the locality from where he came.

So Tokyo is forever expanding but the expansion is often unplanned and haphazard. What Tokyo lacks in distinction and civic amenities, however, is made up for in its extraordinary vitality and variety. Apart from the city center around the Imperial Palace and Marunouchi business area, which present a more permanent aspect of a Western capital city, Tokyo sprawls endlessly into 23 administrative wards of living and business districts and beyond, where more typically Japanese features are discernible.

The average height of a Japanese house is two stories, but the ceiling is so low that a two-story dwelling is not much higher than a single-story bungalow of the West. The construction from wood and plaster is as flimsy as a dog kennel, and is as easily erected as removed. It is remarkable the way the profiles of the busier streets seem constantly to be changing, with old houses disappearing and new ones cropping up almost overnight.

It is a characteristic of Japanese construction that it has no element of permanency. In the wake of an earthquake or big fire, an inhabitant starts building a shack almost overnight. Within a few years the house may be replaced by a more solid structure. The owner of a shop, for instance, will start his business in a small open-fronted structure. He will, in time, if his business goes well, build a better and larger shop in place of the old one. He will again replace this store with a more imposing structure if he earns more money. This makeshift arrangement is very common in Japan.

The main reason for this is that the country is constantly subject to natural calamities of devastating proportions—earthquakes, tidal waves, and typhoons. But the flimsy nature of Japanese construction is also due to climatic, historic, and other conditions peculiar to Japan. The Japanese generally live in close intimacy and harmony with Nature. Due to the sultry heat of summer, a Japanese house is provided with paper screens and sliding glass windows in order to take in the maximum amount of breeze from outside. Life in Japan has always been precarious, what with typhoons and earthquakes and with overcrowding. These disasters are of a forbidding character, and the Japanese would rather live with Nature than try to subjugate or tame it to suit their requirements. This attitude may look to Western eyes like abject submission, but with the Japanese it is the only way to survive—a graceful yielding to Nature, much like the bending of the bamboo before the wind.

An ordinary Japanese-style wooden house is meant to last only about 40 years. Excepting some of the huge Buddhist temples which, though of wooden structure, have stood for hundreds of years, the Japanese have been in the habit of renovating their houses and even their furniture every now and then in order to get rid of staleness, and to introduce an element of freshness into their lives. Thus the Grand Shrine of Ise in central Japan, to which I have already referred, had, up to World War II, been completely reconstructed with fresh timber every 20 years, though the shrine had always been of solid structure.

The Japanese use a pair of chopsticks for eating, but the ordinary chopsticks, unlike Western knives and forks, are thrown away after one use. This penchant for new and fresh things is largely embodied in the Shinto cult which, above all, places emphasis on purity. As a matter of fact, there is a pool of fresh water, usually fed from a well or underground spring, located at the entrance of a Shinto shrine, and a visitor is expected to cleanse his hands and mouth at the pool before he proceeds to the shrine to pay homage.

With the passing of time the Japanese are beginning to build more substantial and permanent structures, but there is indisputably an element of makeshift and improvisation in the Japanese thinking. The recent choice of a site for the new international airport is a case in point. Haneda Airport has become so congested and obsolete that a new and bigger airdrome to take in supersonic aircraft has become imperative.

At first, the government designated a site in Chiba Prefecture seven times the size of Haneda, but the plan was dropped in the face of fierce opposition from local inhabitants. The government decided then to build a new airport at Sanrizuka, some 30 miles northeast of Tokyo, which affords only half the dimensions of the originally projected airport and which will still be too small to cope with supersonic transports ten years from now.

In a crowded country like Japan, it is always difficult to initiate a large construction project involving sequestration of land. But a stop gap measure as typified in the modest Sanrizuka airport plan, obviously is not in the nation's real

91

interests. Not only do politicians lack in vision and moral courage, but the Japanese as a whole have been in the habit of temporizing with small things, without regard to the more permanent future requirements.

Almost total absence of zoning is also characteristic of Tokyo and other Japanese cities. True, Tokyo has its slum quarters, its middle-class residential sections, its upper-class districts, and factory areas. But these rarely exist in separate quarters as in American or European cities. So it is a common thing in Tokyo that an expensive apartment house is built right next to a cheap restaurant, which in turn may be flanked by a fish-monger's shop or nondescript lumber yard.

Thus a variety of people on different economic levels live in the same area, on the same street, and in adjacent houses. Of course the wealthy live Oriental style insulated behind their walls, but just outside are the shacks of the poor. There is variety also in the grades of shops and stores in the same residential district. Then there are ubiquitous bars and eating places at almost every other door. There are today 80,000 bars in Tokyo, a figure which provides the intriguing calculation that it would take more than 219 years to visit them at the rate of one a day!

Tokyo indeed is an endless series of villages. And in each of the villages the rich and poor, peddlers, merchants, and artisans, manage to live together with a minimum of friction. It can even be said that the fascination of Tokyo lies in the fact that each section is almost a self-contained residential-cum-business unit, in which neighbors know each other rather intimately, and a great deal of camaraderie exists.

Tokyo streets, apart from the main arteries and super highways, are notoriously narrow and irregular. But such streets are not without their advantages. For example, take a bustling street with bright lights, but duck right off the street and you find a tiny alley through which a car can hardly pass and along which citizens live in peace and quiet. Obviously there is more practical advantage to this street pattern in the age of the automobile than there seems to be.

Unfortunately the rapidly increasing number of automobiles create a demand for super highways and parking lots. Efforts today seem to be directed more toward the massive tearing down of existing buildings to make way for wider roads and super highways. Tokyo does need some of that and whether it needs it or not, it will happen because the city is growing too rapidly. Yet Tokyo could never be rebuilt in the European or American way merely by widening all the streets to allow the traffic to flow freely and, at the same time, give all the vehicles ample parking space. Tokyo, or Japan for that matter, is much too crowded and too meager in physical resources to permit such a solution to traffic and housing problems. A great deal, however, can be done to improve Tokyo while still retaining its historical characteristics.

Today Tokyo is almost choking itself to death. The metropolis is willy-nilly being forced to expand in all directions. Already Yokohama is no longer a separate municipal entity, but to all intents and purposes a continuation of Tokyo. The city's fast tempo, the drive and ambition of its people, and the overnight changes in its physical aspects, symbolize the metamorphosis which is taking place in the country as a whole. As a matter of fact, the narrow coastal strip along the Pacific Ocean all the way from Tokyo to Osaka is rapidly becoming one vast urban area. A trip by train to Osaka will convince a traveler of this. What little farm land left here and there amid pine groves and on the seashore is fast giving way to factories and jerry-built houses. Village after village, town after town, there is no longer any beautiful and quiet scenic spot left on the entire coastal area, which in olden times was celebrated in the famous wood-block prints of Hiroshige as Tokaido, or Japan's Route Number One, which was dotted with 53 picturesque wayside stations. Instead, on the Tokaido today, one finds almost continuous rows of smoke-belching factories, flimsily built dwellings; and many seashores are being bulldozed into factory sites. The impression one gets is that of an all-pervading ugliness, upheaval, and vitality.

Tokyo is linked with Osaka by the fastest train in the world, which is operated on a specially constructed wide-gauge railroad bed, covering the distance of 350 miles in three hours. Also a super highway is being built which will link the two cities by car in a matter of hours. More and more Osaka is becoming a suburb of Tokyo and vice versa. The whole belt of Tokyo-Nagoya-Osaka is fast becoming a huge urban entity. Some city planners call such an area a megalopolis, in contrast to a metropolis. Such urban development can also be seen

94

in other parts of the world. In the United States an area extending from Boston to Washington, D. C., another zone from Montreal to Chicago, and the San Francisco-Los Angeles region, can rightly be termed megalopolis. In Europe a series of German cities along the Rhine River will eventually form a megalopolis. Only, in Japan the megalopolis is incomparably more densely populated and severely restricted in the space available.

Practically half of the nation's 100 million people live in a mere 1.25 per cent of the country's total area, bearing out the popular notion of abnormal urban population concentration. According to a report based on the tabulation of the 1965 census, nearly 50 million Japanese live in areas totaling 4,606 square kilometers, an area roughly the size of Kyoto Prefecture. Experts predict that by the end of the century one continuous and vast industrial belt will stretch from Tokyo to Hiroshima, inhabited by 75 million people, or some 65 per cent of the total population.

Witnessing this rapid urbanization of the narrow confines of the Japanese islands, one cannot but get the impression that the entire nation is engaged in a colossal effort to generate something that is both modern and Japanese. Yet East and West are not blending harmoniously; but are jarring against each other in the process. One sees for instance, an ungainly Eiffel Tower-type advertisement structure sticking out amid placid temple roofs of the ancient city of Kyoto. Solid, but often uncouth, concrete buildings are replacing the traditional wooden Japanese inns at hot-spring resorts. Everywhere modernization and urbanization are hitting a discordant note, and grate on one's nerves.

The Japanese seem to have the talent to imitate other people's cultural and technical products, a Japanese characteristic so famous or infamous the world over. But it is not in mere imitation that the Japanese find values, but rather in the "Japanization" of imported cultural and technical influences carefully selected from abroad. As a result a totally new creation emerges, and it is in this creation out of imitation that the Japanese seem to excel. The Japanese have in the past adopted many foreign things, as from the seventh to ninth century when there was a craze for things Chinese in Japan. It took many centuries before these foreign borrowings and importations were either thoroughly digested or adjusted to the original Japanese culture. In the meantime, chaos, disharmony, and incongruity have inevitably prevailed.

Riding on a Career Escalator

IN MANY OF the huge department stores which abound in Japan, it is a familiar sight to see hundreds of grim-faced, impassive Japanese men and women of all ages, being silently carried away toward upper floors on an escalator. In fact this escalator ride more or less epitomizes the very life of a Japanese.

Being born a Japanese may or may not be a blessing, but one thing certain is that he or she is up against a severe struggle just to live from the cradle to the grave. In a country where 100 million people have to live in an extremely congested area and where opportunities are limited, the ambition of every young Japanese is to be taken on as a "regular worker" in a government office or business company right after completing his education. To become a regular worker in a big firm, the person is likely to have to pass a written examination as well as an aptitude test set by the firm itself. As for a government job, an aspirant has to pass a stiff civil service examination, for which the ratio of successful applicants is sometimes one in 20. Once taken on, however, he is safe for life because the ministry or firm will make every effort never to lay him off, and will steadily raise his pay according to his age and will train and promote him up the hierarchal ladder of the ministry or firm.

In a Japanese business firm or government office an employee is promoted in principle on the basis of the number of years he has served in his place of employment. Those who were recruited in the same year are promoted and their salaries raised almost simultaneously, and for a younger man to be given a higher position ahead of his senior colleagues is rather an exception. There are even cases of a capable junior official not being given a higher post simply because his former classmates have not yet attained the seniority which qualify them to serve in a higher position. It is only in the top echelons of an organization that promotion in recognition of one's exceptional capability or popularity will take place; for instance, in a big business firm a few outstanding senior staff officers eventually join the managerial class of the firm.

Because of this system of employment for life, a Japanese employer, government and business alike, is most eager to recruit new labor from university graduates. It is unthinkable that a Japanese employer would recruit a worker from a rival firm, or someone of middle age who had served other employers, however capable the latter might be. A Japanese regular worker on his part is not expected to go to a rival firm but is expected to continue to work up the ladder until he reaches 55, which is his retirement age. Once he gets a job, therefore, he is secure in the knowledge that his future is pretty well assured, unless he commits a serious blunder and is sacked.

Here a word or two about the peculiarity of the Japanese educational system may be in order. Soon after the Second World War a drastic reform was effected in the old system under which there were two distinctive phases of education—lower and higher. Higher education centered in the universities, and there were only five state universities and several private ones in prewar years. Lower education was compulsory for all children for only six years, but most of those who finished their primary education went to high schools specializing in commercial or technical training.

The new system, introduced under the occupation's educational directive, emphasized the democratic principle of equal opportunity for higher education, based on the concept of general education and coeducation in all schools, including the university. As a result, colleges and former high schools were all upgraded to university status, which today number over five hundred. This mushrooming of universities has naturally resulted in the lowering of standards, and today there are many cases of a university graduate working as a postman or even as a shoeshine boy in the street. The Japanese even to this day blame this absurd state of affairs on the occupation policy which tried, above all, to democratize the Japanese educational system by abolishing the monopoly of the former Tokyo Imperial University, and by providing young people with a maximum opportunity for college education.

The prewar Tokyo Imperial University had, since its inception, produced by far the largest crop of successful bureaucrats, men of the bar and bench, scientists, and even businessmen. In fact a degree from the University was an open sesame to a lucrative and promising career. However, during the occupation mention of being a graduate of Tokyo Imperial University was taboo with some members of the educational branch of the occupation headquarters. I remember in particular an American education officer who was said to have been a teacher in a junior high school in Nebraska before the war. He was so biased against Tokyo Imperial University and all it stood for that he used to interrogate each and every one of the high government officials whom he met as to whether the Japanese in question was a graduate of the University. If the answer was yes, the American officer refused to interview the Japanese further.

The education reform which was introduced by the occupation authorities was, when taken as a whole, a dismal failure, though the objective of elevating the general educational standards of the nation may have been partly attained. Above all the attempt to abolish the authority of Tokyo Imperial University was a fiasco.

The importance of Tokyo University today is even greater than in prewar years inasmuch as the scholastic standards of hundreds of other newly founded universities are definitely lower, and thousands of the best high school graduates compete feverishly in the entrance examination to Tokyo University, though only a few hope to enter. The proportion of successful students over the number of candidates is generally one in 20.

First-rate business establishments have also been in the habit of obtaining new employees from among the graduates of such institutions as Tokyo Commercial University, Keio University, and others. It stands to reason, therefore, that in order to get a secure and lucrative position, a youth must graduate from Tokyo University or one of the other nationally recognized institutions. It may be mentioned parenthetically that in Japan a graduate of a foreign university is not generally welcome, and those young Japanese who go abroad for a college or university education, have practically no chance of being employed by a reputable firm back home in Japan, let alone by government offices, except perhaps, as interpreters on a part-time basis.

The admission scramble is also fierce with respect to some state-owned universities, other than Tokyo University, when compared with private institutions because of the lower tuition fees and other costs. With second- or third-rate private seats of learning, wealthy parents even try bribery in order to spare their sons and daughters of the grueling entrance examinations. Sometimes the payoffs are made directly into the pockets of university officials who have set aside a few places to "distribute to" as they see fit. The bribe is known to run as high as two- to three-million yen (seven-to eight-thousand dollars) in some cases, but of course at better schools and colleges the only admission price is a grueling examination drill.

If an applicant fails to pass the competitive entrance examination to Tokyo University, he will try again year after year, like the spider which spun the web in Robert Bruce's story, until he is finally accepted, even if it may mean several years' waiting. So tens of thousands of Japanese students who fail in their entrance examinations, wait another twelve months, working day and night, in a renewed effort to be successful in the next year's ordeal. Theirs is a very bleak and demoralized life, for want of any assurance that they will be successful next year. Thus, keen competition for survival starts developing among Japanese youths upon graduating from high school.

In order for a student to enter an outstanding university, which promises every opportunity for desirable employment, he must graduate from a good high school. There are a certain number of high schools which are reputed to be turning out a high percentage of successful graduates. Naturally parents wish to send their children to such prestige schools in preference to others, and the competition to enter such high schools is becoming increasingly severe. Such high schools, on their part, recruit most pupils from certain elementary schools whose instructors are known to be experts at preparing their pupils to pass the entrance examinations to the high schools. Such special elementary schools, again, get their pupils from certain well-known kindergartens. So this cutthroat entrance-examination system among Japanese youngsters starts from the kindergarten and continues right up through the universities.

Thus from a tender age of five or six a Japanese child spends 18 youthful years cramming for one examination after the other. This appalling state of affairs is called *shiken jigoku,* or examination hell, and a hell it is indeed! It has existed for many years, prewar as well as postwar. I used to burn the midnight oil when I crammed for my entrance examination to Tokyo Imperial University, and I can remember during this time that not a few unsuccessful students even committed suicide in despair. Even today cases of educational hara-kiri are not infrequent. Recently in Osaka, a man who lost face when his son was rejected by a prominent secondary school turned on the gas and took his own life. In Nagano City one 15-year-old junior high school pupil jumped from the roof of a department store rather than face an examination hell. I know of innumerable cases in which pupils ruined their health by cramming too much. The high incidence of tuberculosis and nearsightedness among Japanese youths is obviously due to this savage competition. In recent years the scramble for a university education is assuming more serious proportions, taking young lives and sapping the vitality of Japan's youth.

Not only is this inhuman ordeal of the entrance-examination system interfering with uninhibited physical development of Japanese youths, it is also playing havoc with the moral character of the children. Preparation for an entrance examination consists largely of memorizing answers to innumerable hypothetical questions on various given subjects in the school's curriculum. The subject matters covered are so numerous and so extensive that every minute counts. The longer a would-be applicant crams, so much better his chances are of being successful in the examination. So pupils preparing for an examination not only sit up nights cramming as the date of the ordeal approaches, but also cut their meal hours short. One may even witness the curious sight of a school boy haphazardly walking along a busy street, engrossed in reading an examination textbook.

I recently heard that a young boy had told his classmate that there would be an interesting program on television on such and such a night, in the hope that his rival "friend" would waste his precious time watching the television program so that he himself could devote himself to cramming. What a mean and despicable bit of strategy on the part of a small boy in his anxiety to beat his classmate! Thus friendship has become often spurious, if not treacherous, especially among high school boys. A student in his struggle for better marks tries to lull his classmates into inaction in order that he himself alone can emerge successful. It is also said that as a result of repression and abstention for a prolonged period during their adolescence, some Japanese youths today are developing a perverted sexual propensity.

Over and above all these undesirable effects, the examination hell is also seriously interfering with the value of the educational system itself. The examination inevitably leads to an overemphasis on abstract learning, entirely neglecting the practical side of education. The recent deterioration in the teaching of foreign languages is a case in point. Just because English is one of the subjects included in the examinations emphasis is placed on grammar and translation ability, and conversation is entirely neglected. There is also a tendency that once a student successfully clears the hurdle of the entrance barrier to a prestige university, the latter seldom flunks the student. Most courses and tests are easy when compared with the grueling entrance examination. But university education in this space age requires more than just an abstract general learning which, in itself, is of little practical value.

Surprisingly, Japanese employers seem to think that a good education provides only a general background, and is of little use for the specific work the company expects its employees to perform. In fact the company does not expect a precise individual contribution from a particular employee. In most cases business companies employ a new group of young men each year at graduation time. The new employees are not hired to fill specific job vacancies, but instead are put through a routine training period and then given assigned tasks. It is often the case of a young university graduate who majored in law to be counting banknotes for many years after he joins a bank. In fact it makes little difference whether an employee majored in law, economics, or business administration, for him to work in a business firm. In many cases he might just as well have studied philosophy or literature. Only for technical positions are prospective employees required to possess more specialized training, and, of course, a degree in science is necessary in order to obtain a position in a laboratory or a research institute.

Be that as it may, a university graduate, once successfully employed by a government office or a reputable business concern, is assured a smooth journey on the escalator. While the escalator is in motion, all he has to do is calmly wait until he reaches his destination. There is no room for particular individual action, as any untoward activity on the part of the passenger is likely to upset the smooth operation of the escalator. This is one of the reasons why Japanese as a whole are so reluctant to take the initiative in any matter. With them initiative is largely stifled and, generally speaking, the Japanese lack in moral courage and in initiating a reform or innovation.

In postwar years the reform of education imposed by the American occupation has brought about a bitter struggle between traditional and progressive elements. This conflict has persisted even to this day, with violent repercussions— scenes of disorder in universities and high schools and public demonstrations and riots. But, generally, a steady reversion to Japanese methods and ideas has prevailed. Some observers maintain that today as much as one-third of Japan's intellectuals and students are imbued with leftist ideas and ideologies. But it would be a mistake to assume that Japan's youth is forever lost to the left. The radical freshman often grows without quite knowing it into the mildly liberal senior, who tends to become more and more conservative as the career escalator gives him a higher stake in the capitalist system.

The initial salary of a Japanese white-collar

worker is comparatively low. The monthly wage of the 25 million "regular workers" in non-agricultural industries and commerce is just over 40,000 yen, which is about 110 dollars. On the other hand, the standard of consumption in recent years has risen to that of Western Europe. The Japanese are now as well dressed as any other people in the world. Most homes have a television, a washing machine, and an electric heater, to say nothing of other modern gadgets. People throng the world's biggest and most crowded department stores in the large cities where prices are not far below European levels, but where business goes humming along. Thus the discrepancy between income statistics and high consumption of luxurious goods is glaring. The bare figures of industrial wage and salary levels are misleading because Japan is a country where fringe benefits and expense accounts predominate.

There are, of course, family allowances over and above the basic salary, and substantial cash bonuses are paid twice a year at New Year's and in midsummer. Some other fringe benefits include payment of employees' travel expenses to and from work, subsidized midday meals, and in the case of large firms, free accommodation for unmarried workers, subsidized housing for some married workers, and lavish sporting facilities and holiday rest homes are made available. Today a haircut in Tokyo costs as much as, if not more than, it does in most European cities, and so most big companies and offices retain their own subsidized hair-dressing salon where staff members can get a haircut at a nominal price.

Japanese employees, both government and non-government, frequently go on field trips, some in connection with their work, but more often than not on some pretext or other. Nowadays Japanese travel abroad in large numbers but their travels are almost always paid for by their employers or subsidized by the organization to which they belong. This business-cum-pleasure trip can be regarded as another form of fringe benefits. When they go abroad on a field trip, which sometimes may last several months, they are seldom, if ever, accompanied by their wives, who meekly wait at home, for Japan even today is a society still largely dominated by men. It is also the case when employers organize periodic excursions to holiday resorts in the country. Wives are not expected to accompany their husbands on such outings.

Living on an expense account is by and large a postwar phenomenon not only in Japan but in Western countries as well. In Japan, however, the practice is so widespread that it has become almost second nature with the Japanese. In most Japanese government offices and business firms, sizable funds are regularly set aside for hospitality and entertaining. This applies to a big business concern as well as to a small village office. Innumerable small restaurants and other eating places which one finds at almost every other door in the urban areas, thrive largely on petty expense-account banqueting. This wining and dining habit of the Japanese on somebody else's account is essentially the evidence of poverty since time immemorial.

However, in more recent years as a result of heavy taxation and for other reasons, business firms, in particular, allocate vast sums of money annually, not only for entertaining but for every other conceivable purpose which can be accounted for tax free. With managerial people this expense-account spending has become lavish, and on a grand scale. A business executive lives in a comfortable house allotted to him almost rent free which, upon his retirement from the company, will become his own. His chauffeur-driven Mercedes-Benz, his membership dues with several plush golf clubs are all paid for from the company's expense accounts. He can also patronize first-class geisha houses, restaurants, or night clubs, where he simply signs bills to be presented to the company auditor.

Most of these leaders of business or industry are not personally rich, at least in the respect that their American or even British counterparts often are. The manager works through many years of dutiful service before gaining admission to the joys of this tax-free world in which he may revel from 10 to 15 years. But nowadays it is not easy for a Japanese business executive to amass a fortune of his own due to heavy taxation and the inflationary economy of the country. A member of the managerial class is still a small cog in a huge wheel. In Japanese parlance he is called a "salaried worker in the managerial class." Only those who own a big business enterprise themselves in the form of a capital share participation, can be considered millionaires.

Regular workers, other than those of the managerial class, naturally do not have access to expense accounts half as freely as the executives.

Yet workers on a lower echelon do enjoy the benefits of expense accounts in their own way. A foreign visitor, for instance, is a legitimate excuse for up to a dozen members of the firm to have a night out on the town at company expense. Junior clerks of a business firm may entertain a group of Trade Ministry officials from whom the company hopes to obtain an export license, or some such favor, at a sumptuous dinner, and the bill is charged to the company.

So a Japanese salaried man is quite comfortably well off, better off in fact than his wage statistics seem to indicate. He enjoys weekends on the ski slopes, a television, a car, comfort, and security. There is in Japan, however, a large segment of commercial and industrial workers who are more or less on their own and who often work as sub-contractors for bigger enterprises. These small and medium entrepreneurs depend wholly on the output of their hard labor, and are at the mercy of market fluctuations. They have no expense accounts to fall back on. These are the people, along with a vast number of women employees, about whom I will deal with shortly, who help to keep the Japanese industry wage cost low.

Throughout the lengths and breadths of Japan there are a large number of young girls, tending spindles in cotton mills, wrapping attractive packages in department stores, and serving endless cups of tea in offices. Unlike the men, these girls are not destined to move up the escalator, but just to work for several years. This will help them earn a dowry; and the girls will quit their jobs sooner or later after they get married. Since these girls do not move up the ladder and their wages do not automatically go up by seniority, they also contribute to keeping the wage cost down substantially.

When a man reaches the retirement age of 55, he has to quit his employment almost automatically. Those who have joined the managerial class, however, are exceptions and are allowed to stay on for another ten years or so. Though this retirement age limit is rigidly enforced, most Japanese organizations or establishments have some sort of affiliated organization in which those reaching the retirement age can be re-employed. So, the escalator ride continues. For instance, the Japanese Trade Ministry has an "overseas trade promotion agency" which is subsidized by the ministry. Some of the senior officials who leave the ministry are often taken on by this agency. A big commercial house may also have some sort of affiliated firm which could take a few of the retiring officers on as advisors or consultants, which positions however, in most cases are sinecures.

There are also many cases of senior government officials who "parachute" into business enterprises when their government career comes to an end at around the age of 45. They become directors or managing directors in business firms connected with their former ministry, and this second career offers considerable pecuniary advantage. This rather widespread practice is made possible by the fact that Japanese business enterprise in the final analysis has always been dependent for help and guidance on the state, to say nothing of government subsidy.

Such curious continuation of employment may

be explained by the fact that in Japan provisions for social security are still inadequate, if not totally absent. So a white-collar worker has to be employed and paid until he dies, since his pension or retirement allowance is not usually enough to live on in any comfort.

This unique employment structure of Japan obviously has merits as well as disadvantages. Despite what critics may say against this time-honored system, the fact remains that in over-crowded and highly industrialized Japan, this is perhaps the only way of keeping a huge labor force gainfully employed, with minimum friction and maximum security for all concerned. In particular, this employment for life assures loyalty on the part of the employees to the employers, and often fosters a sense of paternalism between management and labor.

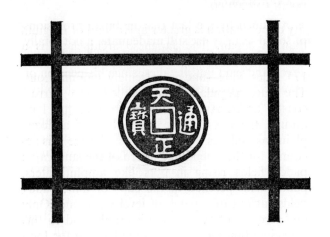

Export or Perish

ANY ANALYSIS of Japan's difficulties, whether economic, political, social, or international, invariably can be traced back to a single fact: "too many people on too little land, too few natural resources." Japan's territory is always likened to that of the state of California, an oft-quoted comparison, with only 17 per cent of the land arable. The population of Japan, which in 1938 was 71 million, a decade later it had risen to 80 million and is now just about reaching the 100 million mark.

These demographic figures alone, however, do not give any accurate picture of just how small and how congested the country really is. Area-wise the Japanese territory is a good deal larger than that of the United Kingdom. Per hectar, the density of population is greater in Holland or Belgium than in Japan. The Japanese archipelago is a slender ribbon of islands—at no point more than 175 miles wide—and is extremely mountaneous. The huge population is huddled into narrow coastal areas. Apart from the belt of flat land around the coast, there are only half a dozen plains as wide as 40 miles across. Hence this accounts for the unending pattern of the landscape: paddy fields rising in tiers like amphitheaters, paddy fields perched in the cups of hills, paddy fields cut out of a patch of level woodland. Only one acre out of every seven is arable, and to this acre eight times as many people look to for food as, say in France. One can perhaps get a clearer picture of Japan's acute population pressure by imagining what Switzerland would be like if that small and mountaneous country were inhabited by 28 million people instead of the 5.7 million as at present.

Lack of living space has severely conditioned the life of Japanese from time immemorial. Everything has got to be on a tiny scale from sheer lack of space—houses, streets, public conveyances, and almost everything else is undersized as judged by Western standards. In 1965, Britain held a big trade fair in Tokyo, which was made popular by the participation of such typically British institutions as kilt-clad Highland pipers and a London double-decker bus as special attractions. Bus drivers and conductors and a full-sized double-decker bus were brought over all the way from England. But, unfortunately, the British bus drivers had a hard time operating the bus through downtown Tokyo to the fair grounds because of low, overhead clearance at every railway bridge and overpass.

Soon after the outbreak of the Korean War in 1951, the American forces met a near debacle and were almost driven out of the peninsula by the communist forces. General MacArthur, then in command of the American troops, blamed the poor performance of U.S. forces partly on the lack of adequate training space at their home base which was the then occupied Japan. Tanks and guns cannot roll on the Japanese countryside without seriously damaging the farmers' precious little paddies. Bridges are generally too flimsy to withstand heavy armored tanks, and overhead clearance of the bridges is also too low to allow their passage.

The Japanese measure land by a unit called *tsubo* which is roughly 3.3 square meters, though officially this time-honored measurement has now been abolished. There is also a subdivision of *tsubo* called *go* which is one tenth of a *tsubo,* and *go* again is divided into 10 *shaku,* an infinitesimal unit. The Japanese official land ledger gives these minute measurements when registering privately owned property.

I have often seen neighbors quarreling over the boundaries of their respective pieces of land. For example, one man may claim a piece of land which is perhaps half a *tsubo,* or 1.6 square meters, as being unjustly encroached upon by his neighbor. The latter, who also claims the ground in question, may put up a makeshift fence to assert his claim, only to have his neighbor tear it down during the night in an effort to recover "his" lost ground. Such petty border disputes are frequent, some of which often degenerate into bloody affairs, though the ground in question may involve only a fraction of a *tsubo*. The land shortage in Japan is said to have helped mold the character of the Japanese people to a large extent. Petty strifes and rivalries, lack of grandiose ideas and ambitions, which are so common among the Japanese, are by and large, the product of their restricted environment.

It is not generally realized just how meager Japan's resources of raw materials are, either. A parallel is often drawn between the postwar economic revival of Japan and Germany. They both had to build new factories from scratch out of the ruins of war. They needed to divert only a small fraction of their armament resources; and even their manpower was enhanced, in Germany's case by an influx of refugees from the East, and in the case of Japan, by demobilization of millions of ex-servicemen. But here the resemblance ends.

Germany could rebuild her shattered economy largely by using her immense coal and iron-ore deposits found in the Ruhr region. Japan is a pauper compared with Germany regarding mineral resources. To be sure, fast-running rivers that drop down from the central mountains yield a fair supply of hydro-electric power. Coal, however, is found in quantity only in the far north and in the far west, and that is likely to run out after another half century. Many of the Kyushu veins in the west are desperately narrow and expensive to work. There is very little top grade coking coal; four-fifths of the nation's need has to be imported. Cotton and wool for the vast textile industry come wholly from abroad. There is practically no oil, and only a meager sprinkling of iron ore. In these and other raw materials most important for industry—rubber, zinc, bauxite, and phosphates—Japan relies on foreign sources to a frightening extent; in all between 80 and 90 per cent of the preceding are imported. Under such circumstances it is obvious that if Japan is to survive, it is to her industry that she must look. A sufficiency of food, and beyond that the comforts of a decent life, can be achieved only if Japan finds the answers to the complex difficulties facing her in production and trade.

Despite manifold difficulties, Japan's economic recovery in the postwar years has indeed been phenomenal. It has surpassed even the widely noted German comeback. Japan has staged this remarkable comeback despite the formidable obstacles of "too many people, too little land, too few natural resources." The key to Japan's success—and her requirements for future economic survival—is the efficiency with which imported raw materials are processed and converted into export products which appeal in price and quality to the rest of the world. Japan's difficulties always stem from her unusual dependence on international trade. More than 80 per cent of Japan's raw materials and 20 per cent of her food must be imported and paid for from export proceeds. This dependence has increased with the rising standard of living which requires increased imports and hence, larger exports to pay for them.

However, the situation has been partly alleviated

by the fact that Japan is now exporting more highly fabricated products than before the war. In fact the face of Japanese industry has been transformed toward the production of capital goods and more sophisticated products, using new techniques developed by the Japanese themselves.

Also Japan today is endeavoring to procure important raw materials as far as is practical at the source. From Soviet Russia to Sumatra and across the broad Pacific to South America, Japanese are going all out to develop untapped resources because this means stabilized supplies over an extended period. Japanese steel manufacturers, for instance, are concluding long-term import contracts with Australian coal-mining interests extending over 15 to 20 years, thus assuring an uninterrupted supply of this vital item for years to come. In such cases Japanese interests are often joining forces with the local suppliers in the exploitation of the sources.

Japanese manufacturers are also in an advantageous position today because most of their factories and refineries are located along the coastal areas, to which raw materials can be delivered directly from overseas, thus effecting a substantial saving in freight charges. The result is that in terms of finished products, the relative cost of imported raw materials has declined. For example, synthetic textiles, in the production of which Japan is excelled only by the United States, require comparatively little imported raw materials. Camera, optical goods, and precision instruments are also export items with a high labor content and require comparatively little imported materials.

118

At one time Japanese exports were confined to a narrow range, competitive mainly because of their low cost. Textiles, toys, and pottery used to be important exports before the war. Now Japan's industrial base is broadening fast and she is already exporting a very wide range of capital as well as consumer goods. This means that Japanese competition is being met constantly in new products—and new markets. This is nevertheless a healthy [1] long-term development which should mean the end of deep Japanese penetration of a few markets on a narrow front.

Thus the specter of "Made in Japan" being associated with cheap and shoddy goods flooding world markets is largely a thing of the past, and if it persists at all, is a legacy from prewar days and is now definitely outdated. The nature of Japanese competition has greatly changed, and the export performance of some Japanese industries has become truly phenomenal.

Growing exports of consumer durables have now induced Japanese manufacturers to establish their own distribution system, usually in connection with repair and other services to customers. This type of export has become common in the camera, sewing machine, and automobile industries. Not a few Japanese exporters and manufacturers have also gone on to the construction of assembly plants abroad, either as wholly owned subsidiaries or as joint ventures, typical examples being Honda Motor Co. in Belgium, Alaska Pulp Co. in the United States, and Pilot Fountain Pen Co. in India.

With its concentration on a few well-engineered

119

products, Sony has done as much as any firm to erase the prewar Japanese notoriety for shoddy, cheap, and imitative merchandise. If anything, the company has put a reverse spin on the old image. A host of imitators have rushed in to capitalize on the popularity of its transistor radios, and one Italian firm went so far as to label its faithful copy "Sonny." Still while Sony does not disguise its Japanese identity in the American market, neither does it emphasize its origin. Prejudice against Japan and Japanese products is still so deeply rooted in the West that it pays not to advertise that Sony is a Japanese brand name. Many Americans do not even know it is a Japanese company. And perhaps that is just as well. Once Sony surveyed a number of American radio dealers, asking them if they had ever handled Japanese radios, and a large majority replied in the negative. But when these same dealers were asked if they ever carried Sony radios, many said yes.

At the end of the war Japanese steel production was about half a million tons. Today the production is over 45 million tons which ranks Japan third in the big league after the United States and Russia, having recently displaced West Germany. Out of the total 45 million tons, as much as one-fourth of Japan's finished output is being exported. The Japanese themselves had not expected such an upsurge in the export of steel products, and were amazed by their own performance. In this industry the fight to make the best use of increased capacity is constantly being waged and the selling effort is backed by some of the world's most competitive prices. Here is a mature steel industry, still in its teens, so to speak, raising its productivity and reducing its use of raw materials per ton of iron and steel produced with ruthless efficiency every year. Japan's coke consumption to produce one ton of pig iron is the lowest in the world, and her shortage of coking coal has spurred on the development of a heavy oil-injection system for blast furnaces. With the rapid rise in her automotive industry, the nation's steel industry is expected to make still greater strides in the next decade.

In recent years ships have been one of the foremost export items of Japan, accounting for about 10 per cent of the nation's total exports. In 1945, General MacArthur decreed that occupied Japan must restrict herself to constructing fishing boats, with the aggregate tonnage not to exceed 150,000 tons per year. Twenty years later in 1965, a Japanese shipyard launched the 150,000-ton oil tanker "Tokyo Maru," the largest merchant ship afloat up to that time. Japan, since 1965, has built more ships than any other country in the world and has been winning an increasing proportion of the world's new ship-building contracts.

The Japanese lead in ship building can be attributed to speed, as well as to quality of construction; the large scale adoption of electric welding before other maritime nations, the use of prefabrication, technical innovations, low cost, and automation. Japanese shipyards cannot only meet firm delivery dates but can even give the exact hour of delivery at the time of signing a contract by the use of electronic computors.

The whole of Japan is being willy-nilly forced into coping with the motor age. Japanese streets

121

in major cities used to be, and most of them still are, only wide enough for a ricksha. Also the traffic hazards of narrow streets are aggravated by telegraph and telephone poles which stick out at regular intervals, making the street more fit for a slalom skier than for a car driver.

Tokyo streets were already clogged with some 80,000 passenger cars in 1960, and I was convinced that a saturation point had been reached as regards automobile traffic in the metropolis. I went back to Japan again in 1965 and was flabbergasted to see millions of cars flooding Tokyo streets, obviously without a serious hitch. To be sure, some of the avenues and streets had been widened and new freeways had been constructed at staggering costs, though most other streets remained pretty much the same as before. There are, however, many ingenious ways of coping with the ever increasing motor traffic. The Japanese have little enough space to live in, quite apart from garaging a car. But now Buddhist temples are letting their spacious precincts as parking lots. In the past many Japanese homes invariably had a tiny patch of garden, but most of these have now been converted into garage space. Many narrow streets have also been made one-way; multistoried parking buildings have been constructed to help alleviate downtown parking problems. One department store in Tokyo has built a five-tiered underground annex capable of accommodating 1,000 cars. Thus, Tokyo and other cities seem somehow capable of solving the problems of urban transit and automobile storage, and one can buy a car without worrying about how to garage it.

122

The whole Japanese economy places emphasis and has strong interests in an ever expanding automobile industry in the future, and after meeting unsatiable domestic needs, the Japanese motor industry is constantly expanding overseas and is presenting keen international competition, not only in heavy transport units but also in smaller and more specialized vehicles. Light cars and medium-sized passenger autos, and even sports cars like the kind that Mr. Honda has been successfully developing, are now pushing their way into the international market. The Japanese motor industry has the advantage of low cost steel and diligent labor. Also most of the industry's products readily sell abroad because of high mechanical merits.

One of the unsavory features of the Japanese export drive is cutthroat competition among the Japanese themselves. If one trading firm starts marketing their merchandise in a certain country with any success, in no time rival trading companies are seen swarming into the same market with the very same item, with the result that the market is flooded with offers at cutthroat prices. Japanese firms under most circumstances compete fiercely and use all the same methods of advertising—special promotions, price cutting, discounts, rebates, and so on. The Japanese government and the traders alike deplore this practice but for the reasons which are peculiarly Japanese, this excessive competition trait dies hard.

This undisciplined competition is also very much in evidence in the fields other than foreign trade and in fact can be said to be almost a regular aspect of Japanese life. Most Japanese newspaper companies maintain regular correspondents in the major cities of the world, not so much for news-gathering as for prestige and status of the papers concerned. I remember that it was the *Asahi* which first stationed a staff correspondent in Geneva, Switzerland some years ago. Geneva has little to offer in the way of newspaper reporting except occasional coverage of international meetings which take place there, such as conferences of the International Labor Organization (ILO) or the General Agreement on Tariffs and Trade (GATT). However, within a matter of years the *Asahi* was followed by seven other major newspapers, which now all maintain regular correspondents there, but most of them languish in the city for want of much to report.

In more important news centers such as New York or London, Japanese correspondents can be counted by the scores. In New York, for instance, there are 26 correspondents, representing large and small newspapers, news agencies, radio and television networks. What a waste of foreign exchange in keeping so many correspondents abroad, when Japan can rely more conveniently on the wires of major news agencies, one may say. Yet the Japanese do not go by economy and rationalism alone. If the *Mainichi* newspaper has a staff correspondent in New Delhi, it would be beneath the dignity of the *Asahi* not to have one in India. Then the *Yomiuri* sends its own man to India. Thus prestige or status symbol is a major consideration in this wasteful duplication of activities in Japan.

There are four English-language dailies published in Tokyo. Apart from *The Japan Times* which has a near 80-year history and which mainly caters to the foreign community, three other papers are run by leading Japanese newspaper concerns. The *Mainichi* started its English edition first, then the *Asahi* and *Yomiuri,* for sheer prestige reasons, came out with their respective English-language editions, and for obvious reasons all three of these papers are known to be running at a serious deficit. Yet the editors and employees of these English supplements are chiefly recruited from among the former senior staff members and other employees of the parent organization and, who, in the event of retrenchment or dissolution, would certainly face unemployment.

This cutthroat competition may perhaps be more injurious in the case of Japanese businessmen, who are often taken advantage of by foreign traders, who can underbid Japanese offers at will. This is particularly the case when the other party happens to be a state-owned organization as is the case with the Soviet Union and other socialist countries. Scores of competing Japanese trading firms vie with one another with offers to a Soviet trading monopoly, which can obtain the best possible terms without any effort on its part. Here again prestige is at stake and representatives of the Japanese trading companies are instructed to get the order whatever the cost, even at a serious loss. This is called "bleeding bid" in the Japanese parlance, meaning that the order received is not commercially profitable and only hurts the exporter. The trading firm in such cases usually covers up for the loss with profits from its domestic sales.

Despite all these obvious disadvantages, excessive competition cannot be deprecated as being always harmful to the interests of all concerned. For one thing, severe competition is conducive to innovation and improvement. Complacency has no place in Japanese business circles. Due to severe competition in which their very survival is at stake, Japanese manufacturers have been able, by dint of constant research and effort, to turn out high quality goods which find ready markets in the world.

When some new sort of industry such as petrochemicals, for instance, becomes the rage in Japan a *zaibatsu* (financiers) group will set up a firm to take part in it; then another *zaibatsu* group will seek to set up a rival company almost as a matter of fact. This has provided the country with a real, if peculiar, kind of competition, in constant modernization. The big firms will often tell you that this is "excessive competition" and that the government ought to do something about it. But one suspects that it is in fact a kind of competition from which Japan has made great net gains in recent years. Duplication and waste so flagrant in their cutthroat competition may thus turn out to be a blessing in disguise.

In certain cases, however, this excessive competition is not left unchecked. Once the Japanese realize that competition is getting out of hand and really becoming destructive, they are ready to turn to an industry-wide agreement on production, sales, and prices, which in the final analysis is enforced by the government. This is especially the case when a certain industry is going through a period of acute depression. In fact there have recently been cases of production cutbacks or even cartelization in such branches of industry as cotton spinning and synthetic fiber production, though some of the measures taken may have been temporary crisis arrangements.

Despite tremendous changes that have taken place in Japanese exports, the bogey of low prices and sweated labor dies hard. Japan's skill at imitation and her lack of commercial scruples, which were prevalent in prewar years, have encouraged other trading nations to treat Japan as an economic outcast, so to speak, subjecting her exports to discriminatory tariffs and quotas. There is a vicious circle here. Japan's industrial expansion and soaring population compel her to find new markets. But the very desperation of her efforts to sell has had many doors slammed in her face. The removal of the stains upon her name has therefore become an urgent necessity for Japan, as she has struggled painfully back into the markets of the world since 1945. Both government and business leaders have made constant efforts to cut malpractices, both through industrial federations and through statutory powers.

In recent years much has been done to improve the situation wherever was practical. Under the guidance of the Foreign Trade Ministry of the government, exporters are urged voluntarily to fix quotas on their exports among themselves. Pressure for orderly marketing also comes from foreign governments or importers who do not wish to see their markets unduly perturbed by indiscriminate Japanese competition. In the case of cotton textiles goods, for instance, Japanese exporters are scrupulously abiding by voluntary export restrictions, but there are still many other fields in which voluntary cooperation is either impractical or where such arrangements have yet to be instituted.

For several years after World War II, Japan was cut off from the rest of the world commercially as foreign trade was conducted strictly under the control of the Allied occupation directives. Not until 1955 was she allowed to join the General Agreement on Tariffs and Trade (GATT), an international organization for liberalization of trade, with headquarters in Geneva. Japan was then admitted to the club, but not as a full-fledged member. Old members led by Britain, steadfastly refused to grant to Japan until quite recently the full benefits of the "most-favored nation" treatment, which is in fact the core of GATT. Member countries were thus free under Article 35 of the GATT constitution to deny trade liberalization measures to imports from Japan.

Ever since early postwar years, it has been Japan's pious hope and pathetic aspiration to do away with the application of this invidious clause vis-a-vis Japan. Newspapers were full of articles on this particular subject and discussions in the GATT meetings in Geneva were always fully reported in the Japanese press. Even the man in the street was vaguely familiar with this notorious "Article 35" as constituting a grave threat to Japan's legitimate trade activities. Mr. Wyndham White, executive secretary of GATT, visited Japan in the early 1950's and later told the story of a taxi-driver in a remote provincial town who, upon learning that his passenger was an official of GATT from Geneva, immediately exclaimed, "Ah, that Article 35!"

Even after disinvoking Article 35, most Western European countries still use a so-called safeguard provision in trade agreements with Japan, allowing them to use their own discretion in placing emergency limits on imports from Japan. Though gradually being relaxed, regular restrictions on imports from Japan are applied by Italy on 104 items, by France on 75, and by Germany on 19.

Outside Europe, Canada applies so-called voluntary quotas to more than three-fourths of all imports from Japan, despite the fact that Japan has always been Canada's best customer, after the United States. The United States, too, which has always actively supported Japan's case in GATT, nevertheless enforces a "voluntary" quota on all cotton textiles, and unofficial quotas on a dozen other items. In addition, the United States also restricts the flow of Japanese exports to the American market by a series of check-prices on many other items. Under this procedure, exports of such items as sewing-machine heads, for instance, cannot be sold to the United States below certain pre-established prices—a price cartel enforced by the customer—which is a new concept in a free world economy!

Thus North American and European countries have always had much to say about the blessings of free trade and the evils of controls. But the trouble is that they do not practice it very well

129

themselves, at least insofar as exports from Japan are concerned. Getting rid of such discriminatory trade practices has been a long and frustrating task for Japan, and it is not by any means at an end yet.

It is obvious that Japan is the weakest of the big trading countries, as she is treated by the West chiefly as a competitor and not as an integral part of the world economy. The problem of access to markets involves Japan in a basic collision of interests with other industrial and developing countries. While Japan will continue to be discriminated against by the industrialized Western countries as a competitor and outsider, it is to these very countries that Japan must look for as her major market. That is where the heavy, massive purchasing power lies.

On the other hand, Japan is regarded by the developing countries as a selfish and greedy trader. Restrictions enforced by a number of African countries against Japanese imports amply testify to this attitude of developing countries vis-a-vis Japan. Hence political freedom of movement to protect her own economic order, while trying to promote a rational accommodation of the different and conflicting economic interests of various nations, is an important task with which Japan will be preoccupied for many years to come.

Hundred Million Customers

JAPAN has perennially been a very poor country. Though Nature has endowed her with a mild climate and fairly fertile soil on the coastal areas, the country is almost devoid of mineral resources and is too small and mountainous to feed a large population. The country, moreover, is subject to natural calamities of all conceivable sorts—typhoons, earthquakes, and tidal waves among others. Under these circumstances the Japanese have never been able to enjoy a very high standard of living, let alone to accumulate any great wealth. Castles and heirlooms of feudal Japanese warlords, who became rich by exploiting millions of their subjects, are paltry and are not comparable in scale and splendor with the possessions of European potentates of the Middle Ages.

131

The Japanese have been traditionally known for their industry and frugality, but the fruits of their labor have often been destroyed overnight by an unforeseen disaster. The early inhabitants of Tokyo, formerly Edo, even took pride in not carrying over to the next day the money earned during the day, for "who knows what tomorrow holds in store."

Poverty, then, has been identified with Japanese life since ancient times. The Japanese have had a strong tradition opposed to ostentatious living. Poverty has even been regarded as a virtue, since it could not have been avoided in a country which is basically poor. There is a popular song which has been sung throughout Japan for the last 100 years, particularly at graduation exercises of schools and colleges as a sort of valedictory song. The song is sung to the melody of "Auld Lang Syne," and starts with saying that "students have over the years been diligently poring over books by the light of fireflies and by the glow of white fallen snow which comes through the windows." Fireflies in this mechanized age have all but gone, but the Japanese countryside in the summer used to abound with these beautiful insects which intermittently emit pale white glows. In days gone by people caught fireflies and kept them in a cage, both to admire and possibly to use as a substitute for a candle. The song serves to illustrate how the Japanese used to live in close intimacy with Nature, and how innately frugal the people have been.

Until the end of the Second World War, Japan's social structure was not much different from the feudal society from which it grew in the middle of the last century. Essentially it was based on frugality and austerity.

When the Japanese economy reached its prewar peak in 1937, it bore even less resemblance to Japan's economy of today than today's economy in Japan does to that presently being enjoyed in the United States. Although industrialized to a great extent, Japan was not a consumer country. Excepting the rich and privileged, the vast mass of the general public was content with few personal possessions, beyond perhaps a flimsy house, some household effects, a wrist watch, a fountain pen, and a radio. Japan's heavy industry was directed almost solely toward building up the nation's military power: its consumer goods industries were concentrating on earning foreign exchange by expanding exports. The transformation which has taken place since 1945, has thus been that of a semi-feudal and half-industrialized state into a highly industrialized country with a politically and economically enlightened population, whose standard of living is now as high as most countries in Europe. In fact today the term "Western Europe and Japan" is being increasingly used in the world's press to denote foremost industrial countries, other than the United States.

Most Japanese industries began to exceed prewar levels of production in the early 1950's, and it was from this period that the great postwar consumer market began to develop. With living costs stabilized and wages steadily rising, the Japanese worker found he had both more leisure time and more money to spend.

As a result the appliance industry was launched

on a large scale for the first time in Japan. Starting with washing machines, the industry soon spread to television sets, refrigerators, and various items of kitchen equipment. The direct results of the appliance boom are best illustrated by the invention of the electric rice-cooker.

Until the early 1950's, millions of Japanese housewives had to get up in the morning more than an hour before their families in order to light a fire and cook the rice for breakfast. The invention of a cheap, simple electric rice-cooker equipped with automatic time switches meant that the housewife could leave it beside her bed at night, switch it on just before getting up and have the steaming rice ready for the family breakfast without rising a minute earlier. Also more and more families are discarding their traditional breakfast in favor of a Western one of toast and butter, tea or coffee, the preparation of which is by far simpler than a Japanese breakfast of hot steamed rice, soup, and pickles.

Similarly the growing popularity of the home refrigerator is bringing about profound changes in Japanese shopping habits. Until recently the ordinary housewife would go shopping at least four or five times a day, making a separate trip for each item because there was no storage space in her tiny kitchen. But merchandising is now being transformed, with supermarkets appearing throughout the country and housewives shopping less than once a day.

The growth in leisure time for housewives, in turn, has brought about an enormous boom in schools teaching advanced cooking, dressmaking, flower arrangement, and various other traditional accomplishments. Some dressmaking schools in Tokyo are housed in imposing ferro-concrete ten-story buildings, and enrollments run into the thousands.

Thus the Japanese people, both young and old, men and women, are at last beginning to relax and are reveling for the first time in what the Japanese themselves call the "leisure boom."

Baseball, which was already popular before the war as an amateur sport, is now big business in Japan. Major professional leagues, modeled after American ones, were formed and popular players are today among the best paid of all Japanese salaried people. Professional baseball teams vie with another in their efforts to engage outstanding foreign, and above all, American players on their teams with enticing offers of fabulous contract guarantees and salaries.

Just why golf has caught the imagination of the Japanese is not easy to explain. In the first place, golf, of all sports, probably has a greater appeal to the Japanese, who live in extremely congested areas and whose daily life is often conditioned by restraint and confinement. Out in a vast open space, which is not readily available anywhere else in Japan except on a golf course, to hit a small white ball to one's satisfaction no doubt affords a welcome relief from the grind of daily life. Also the Japanese are generally deft of hand and, while few Japanese are physically strong enough to drive an initial golf shot beyond 250 yards, most Japanese are adept at handling other intermediate shots, and they also greatly enjoy putting.

The Japanese pursue this royal and ancient game with the thoroughness and dedication which is characteristic of the people. Tokyo and other major cities are dotted with golf practice ranges of various sorts, some built on rooftops, others on small patches of ground in the heart of a city, and fitted all around with ungainly wire nettings which look like twisted zoo enclosures. There golfers of all ages practice, either with or without the assistance of a professional instructor. Most of the ranges are equipped with floodlights and are open at night. Books on golf by famous Western professionals have been translated and are avidly read by Japanese enthusiasts. Many golf addicts try to get the very best imported golf clubs, and the bag also must be expensive as must the rest of their golfing paraphernalia. A Japanese gentleman, his legs usually short and not quite straight, is often seen on the course dressed in baggy trousers, carrying a leather golf bag which is bulkier than he himself. This, I am afraid, is a sight too funny for words.

When Mr. Kishi, a former prime minister, made his first visit to Washington in 1958, President Eisenhower invited Kishi to a game of golf. Not only was Premier Kishi impressed but the entire Japanese nation was so moved and flattered by this act of friendship that the papers reported the event in full, and with much fanfare. A Japanese prime minister being invited by the President of the United States on his official visit to play a game of golf, must mean that Japan is at last being treated on a par with the United States, and that her leader has been taken into the confidence of the American President. Such was the gist of most newspaper comments at the time, and Kishi's visit was heralded as a great success. So great is their love of golf and so deep rooted is the Japanese sense of inferiority toward their recent conquerors.

Golf is not just a temporary craze. It was already popular before the war when there were some 30 golf courses in Japan. Today there are nearly 450 full-sized golf courses throughout the country and many more are being built. The total area of the existing golf courses is equivalent to the entire area of Iwate Prefecture in northern Japan—an amazing fact in this most congested country of the world.

It seems almost criminal to reflect that a land-short country like Japan should allow such extravagant use of the precious little land there is for golf. However, golfing does afford an opportunity to give vent to repressive feelings and, as a matter of fact, no other people in the world take to the game as seriously and as fanatically as the Japanese.

Golf is also popular in Japan as an expense-account pastime. It is a relatively expensive game in the West but more so in Japan. To become a member of a well-known club, "key," or entrance money, which runs as high as the equivalent of 2,000 dollars, in addition to regular dues has to be paid. The average businessman therefore joins a golf club on an expense account of his firm, and a game of golf is played as a legitimate means of entertaining clients or associates of his company.

For many years serious business in Japan was conducted not in an office but in the parlor of a geisha teahouse. Today such talks are increasingly being held in the clubhouse of a golf course. Some businessmen even bribe government officials and others by betting heavily on a game of golf and purposely losing the game in favor of the officials. So the golf craze in Japan runs unabated.

With the younger generation all out to enjoy leisure and sports, skiing has become one of the most popular winter pastimes. A fallacy prevailing in the West is that Japan is a semi-tropical country, and skiing is unthinkable. The skiing population of Japan—that is, the number of those who grasp the rudiments of how to ski—is estimated anywhere from three to five million. Today there is not a single international skiing championship event in which Japanese skiers do not participate.

Numerous skiing resorts have been developed with up-to-date facilities, including lifts and hotels. During the winter season hundreds of special trains are run daily from most major cities directly to the ski slopes. There are a number of ski schools at the resorts, some of which even employ instructors from Austria.

Apart from such conventional sports, the Japanese are now going in for new-fangled sports such as water skiing, scuba diving, and bowling. Popular hot-spring resorts are now as crowded as ever. In most of these resorts traditional Japanese inns of wooden structure have largely been replaced by huge, more modern concrete buildings, the interiors of which, however, retain many of the original Japanese features.

Some of the resort hotels in the mountains and on the seaside are as luxurious as any found in similar European and American resorts. In Japan, though, resort hotels are patronized not so much by individuals as by groups. For historical and sociological reasons there is a sort of inbred collectivism in the Japanese people. It is usual, for instance, that a weekend party at a hot-spring resort is sponsored by a business firm for its employees. The traders' association will hold its annual convention at a resort hotel, or members of a faculty of a university may organize their semi-annual excursion to a hot-spring resort, and so on.

All over the country, school children are seen traveling in groups, chaperoned by their instructor, visiting places of scenic or historic interest. This organized school excursion is a time-honored institution and is a unique feature of Japanese education. A school, say on the northernmost island of Hokkaido, organizes a trip to Tokyo for its pupils. Most of the children would very likely not have a chance of visiting the capital of Japan in their lifetime but for this trip. Also the school subsidizes the trip; special reduced railway fares are obtainable as are special rates for hotel accommodations for the group. The trip also provides lessons in geography and history on the spot.

On the other hand such group activities are undesirable in that the Japanese tend to think and act en masse, depriving them of the opportunity for independent thinking and individual initiative. Be that as it may, the Japanese do enjoy such group activities. Hence most hotels have a steady clientele and seem to be doing a good business all the year around.

Thus austerity and frugality, which have been so characteristic of the Japanese people from time immemorial, are now being thrown overboard and Japanese are beginning to enjoy an affluent society. Such seemingly prosperous conditions, however, cannot be regarded as having been brought about by the nation's farsighted, well-planned design of living, based on sound national economy and saving.

There are as yet many grossly incongruous things in many households in Japan. A family squatting on the *tatami* floor, eating a frugal meal of bean soup, may listen to Beethoven's Piano Concerto No. 5 on a stereo set. Bean soup and Beethoven—indeed! Bach and Beethoven, Cezanne and Renoir—theirs is an art produced in stone buildings with beefsteak dinners in a remote world. Bean soup did not produce them. A young Japanese man driving his own car may live in a ramshackle house which has not yet been provided with a flush toilet. A college student, who has a hard time trying to make both ends meet, may spend the equivalent of 20 dollars to attend a performance by the Beatles.

There is something of an artificiality about all these seemingly improved living standards, and the nation appears to be seeking momentary pleasures rather than the fruit of their well-regulated and rational living. In Japan after the war, many of the traditional values and, in particular, human relations founded on the family system and the restriction of local community, are rapidly crumbling especially among the younger generation. The nation is now generally free to satisfy those desires which, until the end of World War II, had remained suppressed too long.

In Japan, also, asceticism has never been an established tradition as in some of the Protestant countries and the people are now diverting most of their spendings, which they had formerly reserved for seasonal activities and local shrine festivals, to purposes for increasing their enjoyment of life. For this very reason various popular amusements are mushrooming on an ever growing scale, as the agents of commercialism rush to accelerate the continuing search of the general public for pleasure.

As the nation's consumption level rises, helped by the economic growth of a creeping inflationary nature, an atmosphere of great prosperity has been spreading throughout Japan. The Japanese people, once freed from regimentation and also from any sound religious faith, are avoiding a square and rational look at life by addicting themselves to a carefree consumption which derives its attitude from the typically Oriental belief that "tomorrow will take care of itself."

Mass communication media is also fanning this free-for-all spending boom and, as a result, the people have become increasingly engrossed in professional sports or in cheap weekly magazines which blatantly publish lewd sex stories and sensational behind-the-scene stories. The enormous popularity of pinball parlors, which one finds all over the country, and where people, young and old, spend hours on end engrossed in chasing a tiny metal ball for a small stake, is also indicative of an unhealthy trend of Japanese living today.

The poverty of politics and the absence of any worthwhile national goal, are also responsible for this all-out reveling in the so-called leisure boom.

Whatever may be the morality behind this unprecedented consumption boom, the fact remains that Japan's standard of living is rapidly rising and the nation is fast becoming a big market for raw materials, machinery, and consumer goods from many countries of the world.

Meanwhile the younger and better paid Japanese are creating an unprecedented consumer boom. While many of their needs will be produced in Japan, there is a rapidly increasing market for foreign products that are different and good—prestige goods in other words, such as Scotch whiskey, French perfumes, and Italian shoes. Today most of the well-known brands of merchandise sold in shops on Fifth Avenue, Bond Street, or Rue de la Paix, are readily available in Tokyo, at inflated prices of course. The popularity of bowling alleys is already inducing American manufacturers of bowling equipment to enter the Japanese market. The Japanese demand for Western luxuries is so great and so insatiable, that not a few well-known stores of Europe and America are now finding their way into Japan. For example, a famous tailor of Saville Row in London now has its own shop in one of the big department stores in Tokyo, while a restaurant of worldwide fame in Paris has just opened a branch restaurant on the Ginza, the Champs-Élysée of Tokyo.

In recent years the Japanese watch industry has greatly improved and in cheap- and medium-priced watches, Japanese products are fast surpassing Swiss watches. Despite this fact, which is well known to the Japanese, the latter are still buying Swiss watches in preference to Japanese. Such is this blind admiration of those items from the West so ingrained in the Japanese mind. This tendency may be explained by the fact that Japan was for centuries cut off from all contact with scientific progress which even Occidentals follow with intense interest. All at once a new world was opened to Japan as dramatically as though a theater curtain had been raised. The wonders of mechanical invention dazzled the Japanese just as Europeans would be dazzled if they were cut off from the rest of the world for three centuries and then suddenly thrust into the space age from steamship days.

Today Japanese travel in increasing numbers to Europe and America. The returning traveler has to bring back to his family and friends souvenirs of some sort. Japanese etiquette demands this. Often the Japanese tourist buys fountain pens, silk handkerchieves, and other articles in Europe and America. Upon returning home he finds on these items a tiny inscription, "Made in Japan."

Such expensive luxury items as diamonds are now being imported into Japan in increasing quantities. In fact demand for diamonds is so great that a well-known Japanese trading combine has just set up a separate company to deal exclusively in diamonds from South Africa. A few years ago I was surprised to be met at Amsterdam Airport by a Japanese salesman who tried to sell me a diamond. He and one other Japanese were employed by a Dutch diamond dealer in Amsterdam. According to this Japanese salesman, many Japanese tourists were making a point of stopping there in order to buy this precious gem, and his firm was doing good business by catering to Japanese visitors.

To a great extent this improvement in living standards is taking the form of greater Westernization. The use of Western-style appliances inevitably tends to encourage the adoption of other Western practices. Government housing projects are now concentrating on building Western-style buildings, which though still largely jerry-built, eliminate altogether traditional Japanese mats, and living on the floor. As a result Western-style furniture is now increasingly in demand, though domestically made furniture is as yet of such quality and specification that it is suitable for only Japanese use. In spite of this, or perhaps just because of this, there is a great demand for imported Danish furniture, and even for antique furniture, some of which is being imported from Spain, Italy, and other European countries.

Due to the rapid Westernization of Japanese living standards, coupled with an influx of foreign tourists, some of the Japanese hotels are now hiring French chefs for their kitchens, musicians from Austria, while most leading department stores engage a French national as a courtier in their dressmaking department to cater to the more sophisticated needs of their Japanese customers, and possibly to satisfy their vanity at the same time.

A foreign businessman, planning to visit Japan for the first time, should before landing in Tokyo, have proper introductions. A few personal letters to people in the right places can work wonders and save a great deal of time. He should also arrive well stocked with visiting cards, which should give not only his name but also his precise position with the company he represents. The Japanese exchange visiting cards at every opportunity and though this may seem troublesome at first, the custom is extremely useful for future reference, and also for identifying the innumerable people the trader will meet during the course of one negotiation. One should not be discouraged by the slowness, caution, and excessive hospitality which characterize Japanese business. For initial slowness may often be a "sounding out" process, and the Japanese businessman should not be blamed for discreetly seeking information as to the status and reliability of the people with whom he is dealing. Perhaps the most difficult problem is how to tell which is the big man who will have the final say in the deal. Often it is not the top man, for the decision is not made by him but rather by his subordinates. In a big business company responsibility is very diffused, and there is usually a sort of committee which makes decisions by a unanimous agreement after a series of mutual discussions and consultations.

Once a reliable Japanese firm has committed itself, however, there are few more trustworthy business relationships in the world. The complications of doing business in Japan are many but they are not to be confused with the business negotiations themselves, such as delivery dates, prices, terms of payment, etc. When discussions get down to this stage, a Western businessman will find that he and his Japanese counterpart talk much the same language. It is essential, whenever practical, to establish a direct personal relationship with his Japanese business partner, who will feel an obligation to further his business to the mutual advantage of both parties. Once personal contact is established, it should be nourished by correspondence and by further visits to Japan. Once he has established a friendship, he has a friend for life.

Japan, unlike other Asian countries, is singularly free from nepotism and bribery in business dealings. In many of the Asian and Latin American countries, corruption seems to go to the marrow of society. In those countries it is an open secret that when transacting business or bidding for government tenders, foreign businessmen must almost invariably grease the hands of a minister or other high government official in charge, who takes the practice for granted.

This is not to say that such corruption is non-existent in Japan. Back in 1914, the notorious Siemens Affair rocked the whole country. The Japanese Navy in those days used to purchase a great quantity of machinery and armament from Siemens Schukert Co. of Germany. Many high-ranking officials of the navy and the government were involved in a bribery charge and the affair made sensational headlines for a long time. Public opinion was so incensed with the scandal that angry mobs attacked newspaper offices and police stations which were known to have defended or sheltered the alleged bribe-takers. The then government headed by Yamamoto finally had to resign en bloc.

More recently the government headed by Eisaku Sato was under fire for a series of scandals involving a few of its cabinet ministers, in particular, the Transportation Minister who used his office prerogative to have express trains make regular stops at a railway station of a small town which was his constituency. But this latter case is more in the nature of influence peddling than corruption. The fact that these scandals do get wide publicity and an outburst of popular indignation speaks for a relatively high degree of integrity of the Japanese government. In fact, corruption on the proportion as practiced in some of the Asian countries is unknown in Japan. Where corruption in public administration is so deeply entrenched, the news of a public scandal just is not newsworthy as it is in Japan.

In general Japanese businessmen and government officials conduct overseas business more or less according to Western ethics and practices, free of malpractice which is so rampant in the East. In the domestic field, however, petty corruption and influence-peddling is more in evidence, as for instance when local prefectural governments award tenders to private contractors. Also there are cases of flagrant and large-scale corruption where shortage and control systems are in force, as in the case of banana imports from Formosa. It is public knowledge in Japan that by keeping banana-import allocations in the favored channels, a great deal of money is funneled into political party funds. All these things are not unknown in the Western countries either, especially where controls are practiced and politicians are involved. In Japan where politicians are concerned, monetary bribes are almost a way of life. Among the Japanese, however, personal relations play a predominant role, and favors or preferential treatment is almost always accorded to those with whom one is on intimate terms.

I once had a country house in the mountain resort of Karuizawa. There was a piece of land which I wanted very badly in order to enlarge my garden. I had approached the owner of the land in question but he never seemed inclined to part with the property even for an attractive price. However, I found out that the owner was a brother-in-law of a friend and colleague of mine, so I hurriedly went to see this friend of whom I asked for a letter of introduction to his brother-in-law. Armed with this letter of introduction, which in effect was a mere scribble on a visiting card, I went to see the owner who finally acceded to my request, and the deal was consummated. It was noteworthy that my friend did not so much as explain the nature of my intended request to his brother-in-law; all he asked of his brother was to "do the needful," a usual Japanese phraseology, in case I called on the latter. Yet this brief introduction was an open sesame to the difficult deal. The owner of the land on his part merely "honored the face" of his brother-in-law.

This is but one example of how much personal acquaintance or friendship counts in transacting business in Japan. If my son graduated from a university but failed to secure a good job, I would go to a good friend of mine who happens to be chief executive of a well-known business firm and ask him if he could use his influence to have my son employed in the firm. The chances are that my son would be accepted in preference to other candidates who applied for the job through regular channels, provided he was not a hopeless imbecile. In a case like this the executive would drop one candidate out of the few slated for employment. In the Japanese parlance my executive friend "honored my face" by not refusing my request, simply because I was a good friend of his and he was therefore duty-bound to accede to my request.

If a foreign businessman is operating on his own in Japan, or if he happens to be the resident representative of his firm, he will, by cultivating friendships with the right Japanese, be able to do a lot in his business activities. In fact not a few Westerners who landed in Japan penniless are known to have built up a fortune by taking advantage of personal relations with the Japanese, however cumbersome these relationships might have been.

Today economic analysts agree that Japan, now the world's fourth or fifth largest industrial producer, can expect soon to rank third following the United States and the Soviet Union. One tends to overlook the fact that Tokyo has a population equal to that of Belgium, while the population of the prefecture of Osaka alone is larger than that of Norway. With their standards of living fast approaching those of Western Europe, 100 million

Japanese will in the not too distant future constitute a market as vast and as prosperous as that of West Germany and France combined. Small wonder, then, that today Japan has become one of the world's busiest crossroads and one of the most bustling trading posts. Every hour jet liners are flying into Tokyo, disgorging an increasing number of foreign businessmen and industrialists who want to do business in the billion dollar market of Japan.

Once a Japanese;
Always a Japanese

IN MY TRAVELS throughout the world, one of the most recurrent questions put to me is whether there is such a person as a Japanese Jew. There is an English Jew, Polish Jew, and even an Indian Jew, but there never has been a Japanese Jew. There was one Japanese man, as far as I know, who at one time embraced the Hebrew religion but was not officially accepted as a Jew, since his parents were not Jewish. This fact speaks for homogeneity of the Japanese people.

Indeed the homogeneity of the Japanese and the almost complete identification of race, people, and nation is remarkable. The individual Japanese identifies himself more intensely with the nation than does the Westerner who seems more capable of cosmopolitan nonchalance toward national is-

151

sues. In Europe, for example, it is not unusual for a native of a certain country to be traveling with a passport of another country. Some are even in possession of passports of several different nationalities. Such a thing is quite unthinkable in Japan. My son, who was born in the United States, had dual citizenship until he came of age. When at the age of 21 he opted for American citizenship of his own volition, the notice was published in the Japanese Official Gazette of the renunciation of his Japanese nationality. Those of our friends who saw the notice were dumbfounded by my son's ceasing to be a Japanese, and some even insinuated that it was an "unpatriotic" act on my son's part.

The homogeneity of the Japanese race is also striking. Nowadays not a few vainglorious Japanese girls dye their hair in amber or ginger colors and have special facial surgery administered in order to look more like a Caucasian. But the girls will always be Japanese and will never be accepted either socially or racially in Western society. Because of the strong homogeneity of the Japanese people, a lone Caucasian who finds himself among them stands out more as an oddity, and it is difficult for him to be integrated into Japanese life. He will be stared at wherever he goes, and he must also feel ill at ease in the company of the Japanese because of striking physical differences. For instance, he may bump his head against the low ceiling of an entrance into a Japanese house, and his long legs will stick out of Japanese bedding which is tailored to the size of the average Japanese.

152

This extraordinary racial homogeneity is also responsible for the plight of many a Eurasian-Japanese. A Japanese of mixed blood finds it difficult to get employment with a respectable Japanese establishment. At most he can make a living as an interpreter, or if he is talented, as a musician or artist. Half-cast Japanese of Caucasian origin, however, seem to be more easily integrated into Japanese society in postwar years, though social ostracism, latent or otherwise, has by no means disappeared.

During the American occupation of the country after the war, there were inevitably numerous cases of intermarriages and illegitimate births of mixed blood. In particular, cases of children of Negro extraction presented a serious problem. Mme. Sawada, wife of a former diplomat and now a great social worker, has received much publicity for her orphanage, the Elizabeth Sanders' Home, which she opened near Yokohama for Japanese orphans of Negro parentage. She fought valiantly for the well-being and happiness of those hapless children, but there were absolutely no openings for them in race-conscious Japan. Many of the children when they grew up were sent to Brazil to settle.

There are among the Japanese, nationalists and liberalists, conservatives and communists, capitalists and Marxists. Despite the ideological incoherence, Japanese society is uniquely homogeneous. Japan has no troublesome communal problems as in India; no racial disorders as in the United States. It has no disruptive social cleavages; no religious complications. Thus in no other coun-

153

try can one find such complete identity of race, people, and nation.

Speaking of Japanese homogeneity, their eating habits are also something the parallel of which are difficult to find in other peoples. While most other peoples naturally relish their own native food in preference to others, the Japanese rice-eating habit is so ingrained that one can almost say that once a Japanese he or she will never give up Japanese food. Some of the other Asian peoples, too, are inordinately fond of rice. Indians, for instance, are unhappy wherever they may be, without rice, curry, and *chapatis*. But the Japanese attachment to their meal of rice, pickles, and soy sauce is both passionate and even fanatic.

I once knew a Japanese businessman who said all along that he preferred Western food to his own and in fact when he was young, he was quite happy living on Occidental food and even maintained that Western food was much more nutritious and easier to digest. Some years ago this gentleman, while traveling in America, suddenly fell ill and was hospitalized for some time. A friend of his, a Japanese who lived in New York, went to the hospital to inquire after his friend. He had prepared some Japanese rice balls and pickled radish, and took them with him for the sick friend. When the latter received the gift of rice and pickles he was so overjoyed that he burst into tears and was speechless for quite some time!

Some say that with the younger generation of Japanese, eating habits are gradually changing in favor of Western food. This may be true up to a point; at any rate they have been more used to bread and meat. However, their liking of Japanese food is so innate, so ingrained, that I do not see any radical change thus far even among them in this respect.

What is perhaps the most baffling to a Westerner is that the Japanese almost always do things "the wrong way around." When a Westerner expects a Japanese to answer "yes," the latter says "no." A Japanese carpenter starts building a house from the roof down. Also, when he uses his mattock, he pulls it toward himself, while his Western counterpart drives a spade into the earth away from himself. The more formally a Japanese woman is dressed, the more she is covered. An Occidental woman, on the other hand, is less covered when she is more formally dressed.

The reason for this topsy-turviness seems to be that the Japanese character is not oriented toward the presentation of a personality to the outside world, but toward the accord of the inward essence with the nature of the world. In other words the Japanese character is introspective. It is not so much self-reliance as a reliance upon the absolute which is found within oneself.

The Japanese is not demonstrative; on the contrary he tends to repress his feelings, and in a given situation tends to recoil upon himself. A Westerner will loll in a chair with his legs flung out before him, while a Japanese kneels down and sits on his heels. While the Western opera singer strides up to the footlights with dramatic gestures and sings at his audience with the full force of his lungs, the Japanese singer, sitting quietly, sings as if to himself, in carefully modulated tones. The one allows his whole being to flow outward uninhibitedly to his audience while the other, often with closed eyes, makes his innermost soul delicately tremble into song as though singing to himself.

If a Japanese gets an invitation to a cocktail party, he will not jump at the chance to go out and enjoy the function, unless it is within his own circle. He will, in many cases, hesitate and even try to get out of attending the party if he can. Such is particularly the case when an invitation comes from a foreigner. The Japanese, in such cases, says that he will attend in order just to "show his face," meaning that he will have discharged his obligation to the host by the mere fact of his physical presence. Even if he attends, the Japanese does not really enjoy a social function outside his own family or business circles. Hence, a Japanese party host does not have to worry about gate crashers, as is often the case in the West.

As a result of this constant preoccupation with the innermost self, the Japanese approach to their problems more often than not tends to be negative. A few general objectives are put forward, such as the raising of living standards, abolition of U. S. military bases in Japan, the outlawing of hydrogen bombs, more positive "Asian diplomacy," or the establishment of lasting peace. But little thought seems to be devoted to the development of practical problems designed to achieve these obviously desirable objectives. One sees this both in the attitude of the individual Japanese and of the Japanese as a whole. The individual Japanese is quick to criticize the government, but then he tends to sit back in a curiously detached way waiting to see what course the government will take, rather than thinking through for himself some specific policy and effectively advocating its adoption. One might even assume from this attitude that the Japanese government existed quite apart from the common people and was completely uninfluenced by them. Such a negative attitude toward the problems of government may in part be a survival from earlier authoritarian times, but the Japanese people still have not been able to shake it off and to adopt a more positive approach.

Another distinctive facet of the Japanese temperament is that, as a people they are easily warmed up but are just as easily cooled off. The Japanese show a burning aspiration and extraordinary interest toward a problem, but their interest or zeal is not always sustaining. A huge crowd may carry out a mass demonstration demanding the government to lower taxes, or other reasonable demands. But such demands or protests often peter out without any further effective or positive action being taken. The dropping of atomic bombs on Hiroshima and Nagasaki toward the end of the war gave rise to nation-wide indignation only very briefly, and apart from the incessant leftist exploitation of the bombings for propaganda purposes, the Japanese nation as a whole seems to have completely forgotten the bombings. Japanese memories are short lived. I have lived in Poland and knew for myself how tenacious and how vehement the Polish horror and disgust is for German atrocities committed during the war. This is a striking contrast to the Japanese trait of quick oblivion.

Not entirely unrelated to the inward-looking

tendency of the Japanese character is the Japanese trait to keep to themselves. The Japanese, while welcoming a foreigner who comes from abroad with great hospitality, nevertheless feel ill at ease in the company of foreigners. True, the average Japanese makes great efforts to make friends with a *gaijin* (foreigner of Caucasian extraction), but somehow or other he feels everything related to a foreigner is something quite alien to him, and often tries to retreat into his own mental and spiritual domain.

Foreigners, both resident and transient, often complain that they are seldom, if ever invited to a Japanese home. I once lived in a district of Tokyo which may be called embassy quarters. Around my house there lived many foreigners. Every Sunday morning I used to see the ambassador from a West European country strolling around my house. I had known this diplomat rather intimately, and I often saw him walking near my house, apparently with curiosity, sometimes even looking into the compound of the house itself as though he were hoping to spot me.

One Sunday morning I accidentally met the ambassador just outside the entrance, so I asked him if he cared to come into the house and have a little chat. I can never forget the delight and satisfaction with which the ambassador accepted my invitation. In the course of the conversation which ensued he confided to me that during the four years he had been posted in Tokyo he had never once been invited to a Japanese home privately, and his curiosity was at long last satisfied.

The Japanese are exceedingly hospitable, especially toward foreigners. They go out of their way to entertain Westerners even after one casual meeting. But the Japanese almost always entertain foreigners in a restaurant, and often in a lavish way. The reason for this extreme mark of hospitality is that the Japanese consider it rather a lack of politeness to invite a foreigner to their own house and offer him a home-cooked meal. Such an act, in the eyes of the Japanese, smacks of parsimony. In the event that a Japanese has to offer a meal to a visitor in his own home, the meal is often ordered from a caterer and brought in from the outside. A home-cooked meal is usually improvised and considered inexpensive, and as such is not worthy of being offered to an honorable guest. Too, a formal Japanese meal consists of many small dishes and its preparation at short notice is too much for a housewife. So a homemade dinner is offered only to one's relatives or some such intimate friends. Also the fact that after the war the Japanese generally have lived in small and congested quarters is partly responsible for their reluctance to invite strangers to their home. At the same time, with expense-account living becoming more and more the order of the day, there is little chance of a foreigner being invited to a Japanese home.

Whatever may be the excuses for foreigners not being entertained in a Japanese home, the fact remains that a Japanese home by and large is a closed area to foreigners, if only because of the Japanese insularity. A visit of a *gaijin* to a Japanese home is still an event of considerable commotion and excitement. Recently on a Japanese television network there was a very amusing drama enacted by Morishige, a popular actor, and his troupe. One day his affluent upper middle-class family was expecting a visitor from America. All the members of the family left no stone unturned to welcome the *gaijin;* the rooms had been swept and cleaned with care, a full-course meal prepared in advance, and so on. In the household nervous tension reigned just before the visitor arrived, and even a crying child was lulled into silence when told that a *gaijin* was about to make an appearance. When the American finally arrived, a maid-servant got so excited she nearly broke down because she did not know how to address the visitor properly. Morishige, the head of the family, himself, due to his poor command of English, had a hard time receiving the visitor and was often muddled and confused, while the rest of the family did their best to entertain the American with exaggerated politeness bordering on comedy. When the *gaijin* finally took his leave, all the members of the family heaved a deep sigh of relief.

As a corollary to the inward-looking tendency of the Japanese character, their preoccupation with the past may be cited. The Japanese feel and live in constant communion with the past and, in so doing, find the intimate bonds between the people of today and their ancestors. This tradition outwardly at least seems to have been discarded with the defeat in the war. It is true that very few people nowadays keep an ancestral shrine in their own home. Though the cult of ancestor-worship may be gradually dying down, this feeling for the constant presence of the past and intimate bonds with the ancestors is still quite strong among the Japanese.

There is an enchanting festival celebrated at night in midsummer called "floating lanterns" in Japanese. Hundreds of paper lanterns brightly lit with candles are set afloat on a river in order to console the spirits of departed family members. The festival today, far from being discarded, is still being held if only as a summer recreational attraction. It is beautiful to behold hundreds of paper lanterns slowly floating down the river at night.

In the early Meiji period, around 1890 or thereabouts, the Japanese government hired an American lawyer by the name of Denison as legal advisor. He did much to help the government in their difficult task of revising unequal treaties and abolishing extraterritorial rights which Western powers had enjoyed vis-a-vis Japan. Even to this day the Japanese Foreign Office conducts every year on the anniversary of Denison's death a memorial service in his honor in Shinto rites.

Japanese armed forces during the last stage of the Pacific War suffered particularly heavy casualties in Manchuria, Mongolia, and in the Pacific islands. The Japanese dead were buried in improvised graves in various parts of the territories now lost to the Japanese. Ever since the end of the war the Japanese government has been negotiating with the American, Chinese, Soviet, and Mongolian governments with a view to getting their permission for the Japanese families concerned to visit the graves of their bereaved relatives. Popular demands for such visits are so strong that the negotiations are considered one of the important diplomatic matters of the government. And when the permission is granted, the journey to these remote parts of the Pacific islands and also to Manchuria and Mongolia is often not only arduous but very expensive. The Japanese government in many cases sees to it that the trips are properly conducted and even subsidized.

Today, as in prewar years, Meiji Shrine in Tokyo is visited by a huge crowd on New Year's eve and all through the New Year holidays. Also more and more people are visiting Yasukuni Shrine, also in Tokyo, where fallen soldiers of external wars waged by Japan in the last 100 years are enshrined. This phenomenon cannot be construed merely as a revival of nationalism, but rather as an expression of a latent feeling of ancestor worship and spiritual communion with the past, which is still very much alive in the Japanese mind.

The Japanese may pray before the altar of a Buddhist temple and at the same time worship at a Shinto shrine. The Japanese have no qualms about this nor do they regard this dual worship in any way a contradiction. In other words a Japanese can be a Buddhist and, at the same time, a Shintoist. For Shinto is not, strictly speaking, a religion but a cult of ancestor worship and communion with the past. So a Japanese may go to a church and listen to a sermon as a Christian, while in his own house there may be a family Buddhist altar as well as a miniature Shinto shrine, before which the Japanese "Christian" may offer his prayer without impunity.

The Japanese as a people today are not very

religious. Buddhism, which was considered their main religion, has lost much of its *raison d'être* since the end of the war. Some even go so far as to say that Buddhism today exists only for the purpose of conducting funeral rites. In prewar years emperor worship and emphasis on the uniqueness of the Japanese spirit had been propagated with such fervor that they almost served as a substitute for religion. Generally, the Japanese have not been deeply religious, but during the Meiji era the people became more indifferent to the specific value of religion as a result of this thoroughgoing indoctrination in the peculiar form of patriotism. Shintoism also had thus been transformed from a religion into a nationalistic ideology. Hence the large majority of the people today are, to all intents and purposes, atheist and do not embrace Buddhism as their own religion. On the other hand half a million Japanese who have turned to Christianity are more religious in the sense that they go to church regularly, and are generally more pious than their Buddhist brethrens.

The fact that the majority of the Japanese do not believe in any religion as such may have given rise to various strange creeds or quasi-religions to which many Japanese take so readily today. A Japanese needs spiritual solace or support as much as any other person, but since Buddhism offers but little of this except as a ritual, it is not strange that such pseudo-religions as Soka Gakkai, with its fiery proselytizing campaign should be so successful.

Soka Gakkai (Value-Creating Society) is a branch of the Nichiren sect of Buddhism. This religious group has suddenly come into prominence since the end of the war and now has a membership of 13 million, and claims that it is the largest youth movement in Japan. Soka Gakkai opposes "Japan's corrupt and degenerate politicians," and its political party, Komei-to, has already pushed 20 members into the Diet, and will launch a major offensive in the next elections. It is the fastest growing political party in Japan, and can get its candidates elected almost without fail by dint of its close-knit, nation-wide organization. There are many in Japan who fear that Soka Gakkai in due course might emerge as the strongest political party in the Diet and that it might lean toward nationalistic and rightist policies, while others are inclined to think that there is a limit beyond which Soka Gakkai, either as religious sect or as a political party can expand. Moreover, their huge organization is mixing religion with politics and as a result, might degenerate into something which has no great appeal to the nation as a whole.

Another peculiar characteristic of the Japanese people is their reluctance to face reality squarely. If a difficult situation arises, the Japanese would most likely not admit the gravity of the situation but tend rather to underestimate and even gloss over the difficulty. The Japanese language lends itself to this tendency. Japanese is not a precise language like French or English for that matter, but is full of phraseologies and expressions which can be interpreted in more ways than one.

When Japan finally surrendered in 1945, and the country was immediately to be occupied by the American forces, the Japanese never once used the word "surrender" or the words "occupation army" in their official documents or even in the press. Instead the term "termination of war" was substituted for surrender and the word *shinchugun*—literally meaning "an army which has advanced its base," or "an army stationed at a forward base," was used to describe the occupation army. The Japanese language, with its manifold combinations of Chinese ideographs is in fact a convenient language to describe a situation in a euphemistic way, but at the same time is liable to distort or even twist the original meaning. Whatever that may be, this is a reflection of the Japanese mind which does not always act in a logical and scientific manner, but which tends to avoid the unpalatable aspect of a given situation and indulge in vague generalities and, in some cases, in wishful thinking.

After the end of the war the term "economic diplomacy" has been increasingly in use, which however, is also an ambiguous term. It means in effect, that Japanese diplomats should endeavor, above all, to promote economic interests of the country, by concluding advantageous trade agreements with various countries and by helping the super salesmanship drive of Japanese businessmen abroad. "Economic diplomacy" at the same time presupposes that Japan has a significant role to play in the international political arena in postwar years, which is perhaps true.

Japan as a nation is pre-eminently ritualistic. The Japanese stand much on ceremony and are unduly concerned with outward manifestations of etiquette and protocol, which are often carried to absurd extremes. The Japanese bowing custom is still practiced—some bow almost 90 degrees—though Japanese youngsters nowadays may not be bowing half as low as their father or forefathers. It has been my experience that upon my return home from abroad, I find myself kowtowing neither deeply nor long enough to my Japanese friends, for while abroad I had been so used to shaking hands or nodding. Often I finish bowing ahead of all others, and then awkwardly have to start all over again.

Japanese railway stations and airports are always crowded, not so much with passengers themselves, as it is with those who go there either to welcome incoming friends or to see departing ones off. If an influential political figure goes on a trip abroad, there are usually several hundred friends, relatives, and followers who flock to the airport to give him a grand send-off. Naturally the size of the crowd varies according to the standing and importance of the person leaving or returning, but even an insignificant individual may be surrounded by scores of friends and relatives at a railway station or air terminal.

It is difficult, for instance, for a junior official of a business firm not to go to the airport to see his superior off, as everybody else will be there. If the junior clerk chooses to stay away, he will make himself conspicuous by his absence, and his chances of demotion will be greater. So the teeming Japanese cities are made all the more crowded and congested by such meaningless trips undertaken by those going to airports or railway stations to take part in a perfunctory welcoming or farewell ceremony.

Japanese men are invariably seen dressed in black coats and striped trousers when attending an important gathering, such as a wedding reception, funeral rite, or even a cocktail party. A black coat is also *de rigueur* at an imperial household garden party.

When visiting a friend the Japanese has to take some kind of gift. To call on someone empty-handed is considered bad manners. Apart from occasional gift-giving the Japanese distribute or exchange gifts twice a year—at the end of June and at New Year's. Employees buy presents for their employers, officials take seasonal gifts to their superiors, school children's parents send suitable presents to the teachers, businessmen distribute gifts to their clients, and so on. Gifts range from a box of candy to costly items such as transistor radios, pearl necklaces, and even automobiles, depending on the importance of relationship between the gift-giver and the recipient.

The custom is so prevalent that in June and December of each year the nation goes all out on a frenzied shopping spree. Most big department stores have an efficient delivery service and do a roaring business. Often a high-ranking government official of the finance or trade ministries ends up filling an entire room with presents received from numerous associates or business contacts. Some of these officials cannot possibly hope to use these goods themselves and so dispose of the items and realize a handsome fortune. It is also said that most Japanese politicians of note do not have to

167

buy their foodstuff from grocers at all, as they constantly receive presents of seasonal food items, canned food, imported wines and spirits, from their friends and followers.

This seasonal gift-giving is a time-honored custom, which even in this mid-20th century dies hard. It is difficult for a Japanese not to conform to this inveterate custom without making himself an object of suspicion, if not ridicule, of all concerned.

The Japanese custom of exchanging New Year's cards is also both time-honored and extensive. It is not to be compared with the exchange of Christmas cards in the West. In Japan not only one's close friends but also his acquaintances, former associates, and almost anyone else with whom he may have had any contact at all, send greetings. At the end of the year, therefore, tremendous time and energy is consumed in sending out New Year's greetings and the strain on the postal service has, in recent years, almost reached the breaking point. While the custom of exchanging season's greetings is a pleasant one, the Japanese custom is sometimes too perfunctory. But such is the extent of Japanese conformitism and their anxiety to keep up with the set pattern of life.

Thus one can see that human relations are enormously important in Japanese life. It is difficult to define the quality of Japanese friendships. In the first place they are more intimate and emotional than the friendships among foreigners. Of course in all friendships affection plays a great part, but with the Japanese when one begins liking people one gets very much involved with them. The Japanese extend an intense personal loyalty to those who are their friends. One finds himself giving a great deal of himself in emotional terms. Sometimes it is a strain, and one finds oneself craving for those detached, half-tone friendships which are so frequent among Occidentals.

Thus the Japanese live under constant mental restraint and preoccupation with their friends and neighbors, and human relations can be said to be much more cumbersome than is perhaps the case with other peoples. The Japanese life is, as yet, largely conditioned by a feudalistic pattern and is characterized by the absence of individualism which is the basis of Western society.

Hence, there are not a few Japanese who long to be freed from the meaningless customs and cumbersome practices which attend Japanese society. I have known in a remote village in British Columbia, a Japanese immigrant family who made a living by farming and who refused to have anything to do with the Japanese community of the district. It was pathetic to see how all members of this particular family tried to live like Westerners, by discarding rice-eating, Japanese New Year's, and other festivities, and above all by avoiding the company of their compatriots. Another time I met a Japanese expatriate businessman in New York who, when his firm ordered him back home, bemoaned the fate of being a Japanese with genuine feeling.

1868 and All That

JAPANESE history dates back to 660 years before Christ, and though the early history is shrouded in hoary tales of the sun goddess and other legendary figures, a generally accepted belief is that several powerful families in the western part of Japan formed a primitive empire in the latter third or early fourth century. They chose an emperor and set up the Yamato Court, and the imperial lineage has been unbroken ever since and the present emperor is the 124th of the same dynasty. Yamato is the ancient name of Japan and also of Nara Prefecture where the court was first established.

The Yamato Court expanded its sphere of influence to the western region of the country and, at one time, as far as Korea across the sea. The opening of intercourse with Korea brought Chinese learning, Confucianism, and Buddhism to Japan from the fourth century onward. Such continental culture had a great influence upon the creation of Japan's own culture. The influence of Buddhism was particularly strong under the patronage of the Imperial Court.

The seventh century saw the flowering of Buddhist culture in Japan in the development of the art of temple architecture and of Buddhist image casting, as exemplified by the Horyu-ji Temple built in Nara in 607. In 710, the Yamato Court moved its seat permanently to Nara. Prior to this move it was customary to transfer the seat of the court from place to place whenever a new emperor came to the throne.

Nara was the first permanent capital of Japan, and remained so for about 150 years, during which time there were seven successive imperial reigns. This period is called the Nara period and during this era there was a significant growth of arts and sciences as a result of increased intercourse with China. Many temples were built and the great bronze statue of Buddha was cast and enshrined in the Todai-ji Temple in 743, which has been preserved to this day.

In 794, the capital was moved from Nara to Kyoto and a glorious dynastic age with Buddhist culture and court literature, represented by Lady Murasaki's *The Tale of Genji,* flourished, lasting 400 years. This period is known as the Heian period (794–1192). The Fujiwara family took the helm of state affairs from 858 to 1086 at which time it lost power by the rise of local warriors all over the domain. The Taira clan then held sway, but was finally overthrown by the rival Minamoto clan in 1185. Yoritomo, the lord of the winning clan, became shogun, or military dictator, in 1192 and established his shogunate government at Kamakura.

Warrior government began at that time, and by usurping the power of the emperors, lasted nearly 700 years, being taken over by different conquerors until the Imperial Court came back to power in 1868. From the 14th century to the beginning of the 17th, the country was divided into the domains of different war lords, and internecine civil warfare was the order of the day. This prolonged period of warring chieftains did much to mold the character of the Japanese people of today. Though courteous on the surface, the Japanese are unable to really trust each other and are bent on undermining others whenever the opportunity presents itself. The so-called excessive competition of Japanese traders among themselves, which hurts everyone concerned, is greatly reminiscent of this incessant civil war period.

In 1603, Tokugawa Iyeyasu became shogun and set up his government in Edo, the present-day Tokyo, while the Imperial Court remained in Kyoto. The Tokugawa family reigned for nearly 250 years and, due mainly to their clever manipulation of various local chieftains, were successful in ensuring peace in the country. The Tokugawas hermitically closed the country to the outside world out of fear of European aggression. Of course a tiny bit of Western learning, products, and intelligence did trickle through the Dutch settlement near Nagasaki into Japan, but during

172

the entire period of the Tokugawa shogunate all things foreign were strictly controlled by the government, and any Japanese trying to go abroad did so at the risk of capital punishment.

It is generally believed that this isolation policy resulted in stifling Japanese ambition for expansion abroad in later years. It is also noteworthy that during the three centuries of isolation from the rest of the world, the Japanese could develop art, literature, and commercial activities under peaceful conditions. It is also open to question that but for this rigid ban on foreign intercourse Japan might have come under some sort of foreign domination, the fate that befell most other Asian countries.

In any event, since the early and mid-19th century, the visits of European ships to Japanese shores had become more frequent, and the Tokugawa shogunate government found it increasingly difficult to adhere to the isolation policy. The visits of the American fleet under Commodore Perry (1853–54) finally led to the opening of the country to the world in 1858. This decision made by the Tokugawa government without the consent of the Imperial Court spurred the anti-shogunate movement among the imperialistic feudal clans. In 1867, the 15th Tokugawa shogun returned the sovereign power to the throne, and in 1868 the Edo castle, the present Imperial Palace in Tokyo, was unconditionally surrendered to the Emperor's army consisting of imperialist clansmen. Nearly 700 years of warrior government thus came to an end.

The year 1868 was of great significance for

Japan. The chronological name was changed from Keio to Meiji, Edo was renamed Tokyo, and the capital of Japan was transferred from Kyoto to Tokyo. This great political event is called the Meiji Restoration, and marks a significant starting point of modern Japan.

The nation welcomed the new regime with the greatest expectations. The immediate consequence of this restoration was a radical change in Japan's relations with the outside world. Japan became the eager pupil of the Occident, and Westernization was the order of the day. The government started sending delegations and students abroad to learn the techniques and sciences of Western countries on a large scale, and most systematically.

Students were chosen with great care and the countries to which they were to be sent were selected with equal care. They went to England to study the navy and merchant marine, to Germany for jurisprudence and medicine, to France to learn silk filature. The first official mission ever sent to the United States was headed by Prince Iwakura in the year 1870 or thereabouts. When the delegation arrived in San Francisco, the members were invited to dinner by the local Americans. Toward the end of the dinner ice cream was served, which the Japanese greatly enjoyed as they had never tasted such a cool and delectable dish before. One of the Japanese guests took out a pad of tissue paper from his pocket and secretly wrapped up a leftover portion of the ice cream in the paper, hoping to eat it when he got back to the hotel!

Never in the history of Japan had there been

such a period of extensive learning from abroad. The Meiji era may perhaps be compared to that great period from the sixth to the ninth century when the Japanese imported Chinese civilization. In this manner Japan went all out in the early Meiji years to learn what the West could offer in all fields, and there was a craze to copy all things Western.

This was called the age of "civilization and enlightenment," *bummei kaika* in Japanese, the most notable example of which was the imitation of Western high society at a European-style club house called the Rokumei-Kan in Tokyo, where noblemen and other upper-class Japanese congregated, attired in the most fashionable of Western dress—men in tails and white tie, women in décolleté—to indulge in Western ballroom dancing under brightly lit chandeliers. Named after this social club, the early Meiji era was popularly known as the era of Rokumei-Kan. Thus the modernization of Japanese society had gone ahead with amazing rapidity.

Most statesmen of the early Meiji era were men of outstanding personality and competence. They promulgated a constitution which was based on the unquestioned authority of the emperor, the Japanese counterpart of the "divine right of kings." As time went on, this rationalization of imperial power gave rise to emperor worship and contributed to the political consolidation of Japan to a remarkable degree.

In 1891, Emperor Meiji published his famous *Rescript on Education* which laid emphasis on absolute devotion of the Japanese people to the cause of the nation, and which was instrumental in orienting school education toward intense nationalism. The Ministry of Education ordered each school to preserve a portrait of the Emperor and a copy of the *Rescript on Education;* the national anthem was to be sung on all national holidays. The unveiling of the Emperor's portrait and the recitation of the *Rescript on Education* became the compulsory ceremonies on many important occasions. I remember when I was a boy a fire broke out in an elementary school near where I lived. The headmaster of the school plunged into the flaming building to save the portrait of the Emperor, but was too late and perished in the flames. This incident was heralded at the time as a patriotic act of the highest order. In this way nationalism began to possess a religious fervor and the nation was dedicated more than ever toward making Japan one of the strongest powers of the world.

The leaders of the early Meiji era also recognized that the military position of the country was conditioned by its general development, which led to the policy reflected in the slogan of *fukoku-kyohei*—a rich country and a strong army. Their modernization program included not only the organization of a new state but also the creation of a strong army based on compulsory military service, a new education system which aimed at compulsory education, and an industry equipped with Western machinery and techniques. In other words, the program envisaged not only the creation of a political order but also of a new economy by the induction of Western production methods.

Soon after the Restoration the government set up industrial establishments such as cement factories, cotton spinning mills, and steel works, which were to serve as models. The government imported machinery which was sold to entrepreneurs on deferred payment bases. The important mines were worked by the state with the help of foreign engineers and imported equipment. The state was particularly active in the field of transportation, and railways were a state monopoly then as they are today. The government bought a number of ships from abroad and heavily subsidized both domestic and ocean-going shipping.

These enterprises started by the state were later sold to private entrepreneurs at very low prices and a large part of them were acquired by financiers who later came to be known as *zaibatsu* which formed the leading class of Japan's economic society. Thus the state laid the very foundation of modern capitalism in Japan, and it is noteworthy that the government even to this day has been instrumental in influencing the industrial and economic development of the country to an extraordinary degree.

Japanese businessmen look to the state for help when mismanagement or business depressions threaten to ruin the industry. Since 1868 "relief" actions by the government, usually financed through the Bank of Japan, have become standard procedure in times of crises. This system is partly responsible for the tendency of Japanese businessmen to lose sight of realities of the market and to act sometimes in an easygoing and irresponsible manner. This undue intervention of the state in building a modern capitalist economy was also necessitated by the fact that Japan had to wage two major wars, first against China and then Russia, in the course of 40 years after the Restoration, and the country could not afford simply to pursue economic objectives for economic reasons.

Under the slogan "a rich country and a strong army," Japan had to sacrifice the economy in order to build her military might. It was obviously impossible to finance the enormously expanding productive machinery and the huge military expenditures solely out of savings. The government therefore had to resort to the crude method of an unlimited issue of bonds and paper money, and the industrialists on their part could, in the long run, wipe out their heavy borrowing from the state or the Bank of Japan as a result of an inevitable currency depreciation. In fact, ever since 1868, the Japanese economy has been characterized by a mild inflationary trend, and the predilection of Japanese financiers and politicians for the easy road of credit expansion has persisted to this day.

The *zaibatsu,* which could be translated as "financial clique," were the rich families of prewar Japan, such as Mitsui, Mitsubishi, or Sumitomo, which came to control the great industrial and commercial empires. But it was in the early Meiji era that the *zaibatsu* really began to grow into what they are today, and to form close connections with politicians and the government.

After the Second World War, the Americans, with reforming zeal, split up the firms in these massive empires into individual entities, but this was like grappling with a jelly fish, for the cohesion trait has remained. They are secure again today by interlocking directorships and high-level executive consultations among the firms that used to be connected with the old groups; by interlocking shareholdings among group members, and by the fact that one of the big city banks—several of which are successors of old *zaibatsu* banks—is holding a central position in each group.

These great Japanese trusts and monopolies are not exactly in the same form as in Meiji days; for one thing there is no influence or pressure on behalf of an armaments industry. Also they are no longer family enterprises as when they were founded. Yet these huge complexes and organizations have, after the war, contributed much to the expansion of Japanese industry, merchandising, the import-export business, and merchant banking.

The oldest of the companies in international trade is Mitsui Company. The Mitsui family started business more than 300 years ago, and now claims to be the largest and most comprehensive group in Japan, and possibly in the world. It handles from vitamin pills to atomic reactors. Mitsui promotes overseas trade by acting as financier, merchant bank for export loans, and as a partner in joint selling ventures.

When the Pacific War broke out on December 7, 1941, the American authorities forthwith impounded the New York office of Mitsui Company. The officials who seized and examined the books of Mitsui's New York office at the time were flabbergasted by the enormous volume of trading which had been carried out by the company, not so much between Japan and the United States, but with other countries as well. The officials were said to have exclaimed that as an international trader, Mitsui was by far the largest, most unique organization, the like of which had never existed in the United States, let alone anywhere else in the world. In fact I remember that in prewar years Mitsui operated in India on a grand scale; they used to buy up jute which they sold to Australia and other countries, and the company's operations nearly controlled the jute market of India.

Mitsubishi Trading Co. was founded in 1870 by the shipping family Iwasaki who controlled the famous N.Y.K. steamship company. Apart from the trading company there are 36 related Mitsubishi companies with their own capital and management.

The third in the *zaibatsu* line is the Sumitomo group of Osaka which works the same bewildering range of activities as its two big competitors, with the same division of energies between import and export, domestic and foreign trade. Such trading houses as Mitsui, Mitsubishi, and Sumitomo, among themselves conduct more than four-fifths of Japan's overseas' trade today, and the proportion is growing. Thus *zaibatsu,* essentially a product of the Meiji era, is almost a symbol of Japan's economic development.

Another remarkable achievement of the Meiji period was the creation of efficient administrative machinery. The leaders of the new reign, however, did not create its bureaucracy from scratch, but rather inherited the highly centralized Tokugawa government machinery almost intact. The Japanese as a whole are prone to receiving orders from above and bureaucracy came naturally to them. But for the efficient machinery of bureaucracy, Japan, since the Restoration, could not possibly have achieved what she set out to do; namely, to make Japan a foremost military and industrial power. Japan has perpetuated her efficient civil service to this day and the curious thing is that whenever the caliber of the political leaders deteriorated, the civil service always maintained its integrity and high competence.

Japan's emergence as a modern nation is generally identified with her development since the Meiji Restoration of 1868. Ironically enough though, the fanatical devotion to the emperor and blind faith in the superiority of the Japanese nation which had been exalted to a religious fervor by the leaders of the Meiji era, were to prove in later years partly responsible for the disastrous defeat of Japan in World War II. The heavy nationalistic and militaristic indoctrination had since paved the way for the rise of the totalitarian militarists who first embarked on adventures on the Asiatic continent and finally plunged the nation into the Pacific War.

On the debit side of the Meiji reforms, mention must be made of the failure to foster a truly democratic government in a modern state. To be sure, the Meiji reformers concluded from their study of Western political institutions that a constitution was essential to a modern state and that some form of parliamentary government was also a necessary adjuncture of the political machinery.

The Japanese Constitution was therefore promulgated in 1889 which, however, provided for the emperor being the fountain head of all authority in the state and for his absolute right to rule. The Diet, or a parliament, composed of an upper and lower house, was to be established— the House of Peers modeled after the British House of Lords, and the House of Representatives to be elected by men past a certain age, supported by the paying of a stipulated annual tax. In 1890, the first elections were held but only about one per cent of the total population had the right to vote, and the Diet was far from being a representative government.

Meanwhile, the younger founders of the new regime, now grown to middle age, still continued to control Japan and several of those illustrious leaders of the early Meiji era had become "elder statesmen," who advised the emperor on the appointment of a prime minister, or on other important matters.

In this way the Japanese Diet was only a façade of the country's Westernization, and in spirit the government had hardly departed from the traditions of a paternalistic and authoritarian state. It is a sad commentary on the Meiji Restoration that the tremendous strides made both in military and in economic fields in so short a period were made possible only by dint of a totalitarian rule, and there was hardly room for fostering a genuinely democratic government. At the same time it was obviously impossible to change a docile people overnight who, over the centuries, had been

182

imbued with feudalistic ideas and who were so used to authoritarian rule.

In many ways the present-day Japan seems to be carrying on what has been achieved since the Restoration. True, chauvinistic patriotism of the Meiji period has completely disappeared. But a phenomenal economic development such as was achieved during the Meiji era is once more being re-enacted since the close of World War II. The Japanese are again visiting Europe and America in large numbers in their desire to copy, admire, and to learn what is best in the Western civilization. The truly democratic form of government, which the leaders of the early Meiji era failed to establish, is still in the process of being evolved. All in all, the Japanese people have the virtues, shortcomings, and qualities, which once given an impetus, are capable of achieving something which is truly astounding.

Democracy—Japanese Style

FOR MANY centuries before World War II, emperor worship and the family system were the most influential environmental factors in the formation of the Japanese personality and basic attitude. From time immemorial great importance has been and still is placed on the family unit rather than on the individual. The family was headed by the patriarch, and members of the family were expected to behave in ways befitting their standing.

They were neither allowed to act beyond that limit nor permitted to entertain personal desires which were not in accordance with the family's standing. Children had to obey their parents' bidding, however unreasonable it might have been, and it was through this obedience that the unit of the patriarchal family was maintained. Thus in many families it was customary for the father or the grandfather to have the privilege of using the family communal bath before any other family member, and the biggest helping of *sashimi,* or sliced raw fish—the much-prized and expensive Japanese delicacy—was served first to the family head at dinner.

Though the family system has disintegrated to a large extent since the war, family unity is still strong in Japan, as may be seen in the case of marriage, which has to take into account various family considerations above everything else. The concept of the family or community is an essential part of the Japanese personality and way of life. The Japanese do not recognize the fiction of an isolated individual whose honor is merely a matter of his own concern.

Children are told by their parents and teachers not to do this or that for fear that "others may laugh at you." Indeed this is one of the cardinal points of Japanese upbringing. Thus from the earliest youth the Japanese avoids the danger of being laughed at by behaving as unobtrusively as possible in public. He approaches others with a courteous smile, but veils himself in an atmosphere of secrecy, even when there is nothing to be hidden. While very young children are allowed comparative freedom, they are forced to restrain themselves as they grow older. In this way the Japanese' spirit of independence is nipped in the bud. In Japan one often witnesses a street scene in which, when a small child falls down he does not make an effort to stand up by himself, but keeps on crying until his mother or someone else comes to his rescue.

In Japan babies are not brought up as they are in the West. A baby, upon his birth, is not put on a feeding or sleeping schedule. The fact that playpens or cots are not generally in use, may in part be responsible. When a baby starts fussing before bottle time or bedtime, his mother in most cases accedes to the wishes of her baby. If the baby puts his fingers in his mouth, or sucks his thumb, his mother will not slap his hand or try to break him of this habit. Thus no firm discipline is applied toward the infant from his birth until he is fully grown. Pampering of children is a result of an inordinate love of children by the Japanese, but the children's wishes and desires are often ignored and made light of in the family system in which the parents play a dominant role. The wishes of children are often restrained with such reasons as: "You cannot go to a college since you are not the son of a rich man, like Mr. A," or "Look at B who comes from a poor family."

In view of the peculiar social stratification the parents naturally wish their children to rise as high as possible for the family's sake. And in order to be successful in life in a country with limited opportunities, it is important that the end should justify the means. So the Japanese parents often make their children do things much against their will. This mentality is largely responsible for the cutthroat competition which is so prevalent today among the students who want to enter the very best universities that often subject them to grueling and inhuman cramming ordeals for entrance examinations. Often the desire to enter a prestige college or university is not so much that of the student himself, as it is for the sake of his parents' vanity.

In prewar times the Japanese character received additional molding in schools which gave instructions in morals, the main emphasis being placed on serving the country as faithful subjects of the emperor. This absolute obedience to authority has done much to stifle individual initiative, and has given rise to the uniformity of action and thinking among the Japanese.

The Japanese character has thus been formed in a social environment which forced people from the time of their birth onward to maintain their own social standing and to respect their relationships with others. The family system turned out men who could live, above all, in harmony with their environment. The Japanese attitude toward life, then, is characterized by inertia and by submission to authority, rather than by individual conscience or rational judgment. This condition reflects basically a lack of independent spirit and individual initiative. Men who live amid such conformity and uniformity tend to become opportunistic and their actions gain general acceptance by the very fact that the majority of people act in the same way. The beaten path is the safest and since the individual seldom, if ever, acts according to conscience, an action motivated by the latter could result in isolating him from the majority.

In a well-known restaurant in Hong Kong a headwaiter once told me that no nationality is easier to serve than the Japanese. According to this waiter, Japanese diners, especially when they are in a group, do not bother to look at a menu but select the dishes themselves. If someone in the group makes the choice of say, a noodle soup and sweet-sour pork, the rest of the group will follow suit as if in unison. This tendency to follow somebody else's choice is also evident in a Japanese restaurant in Japan, where the menu is written in Japanese.

In a Japanese office or organization, if any decision is required, the first thing for the party concerned to do is to refer to the precedents. Then discussions follow among those concerned on the basis of the precendents without any immediate action being taken. Usually a suggestion as to a possible course of action to take is made and submitted to their superiors, who may approve of the suggested action. Thus the Japanese attitude is to drift with the tide, and nobody really makes a decision. What appears to be a decision is nothing but an anonymous consensus. As a result, the Japanese can be said to be essentially conservative, and seldom plunge into rash action.

The Japanese are inordinately fond of *zadan-kai,* a sort of round-table discussion. In Japanese newspapers and periodicals one often reads of the accounts of such discussions which range over all conceivable subjects. At such discussion meetings usually three or more persons take part and there is a master of ceremonies who merely conducts the proceedings. Take, for instance, a *zadan-kai* on the Vietnam situation. Several prominent publicists are invited to take part in the discussion. Each of the participants at the request of the M.C. is invited to express his views on the subject but few, if any, venture really independent or original views or ideas. If A starts the discussion, B who follows, often endorses or contradicts the remarks made previously by A, without himself expressing his own independent idea. B is followed then by C who also prefers not to come out with his original idea but rather tries to toy with the remarks so far made by A and B. Thus the discussion goes on without any conclusion being reached or any consensus being taken. When the discussion has lasted for some time, and the audience has had enough, the M.C. will wind up the meeting by merely announcing that it is about time to stop the discussion. This panel-discussion example is typical of Japanese reluctance to take the initiative, and reveals their opportunistic attitude and their tendency to avoid responsibility.

Closely related to this Japanese characteristic is the lack of ego on the part of the Japanese. In fact this latter characteristic is a direct result of stifling one's initiative and independent thinking. Not long ago at the University of California several foreign students were holding a discussion on world leadership. A Japanese youth in the group declared that "after World War II it is the United States which has assumed leadership in the world." There were German, Egyptian, and Hungarian students in the group, all of whom took strong exception to the Japanese student's statement. They argued that the fact that the United States helped rehabilitate Europe by giving massive aid under the Marshall Plan did not necessarily mean that the country assumed either moral or spiritual leadership among the nations of the world since the war. The Japanese student, on the other hand, was, perhaps due to the American occupation of his country, so overwhelmed and awe stricken by the United States that he could not assess the situation in a more objective manner.

The Japanese by nature are shy and humble and are not sufficiently self-assertive. They easily succumb to superior forces surrounding them. A Japanese who goes to America to study or work often likes to assume an English Christian name in the place of his own. Some even try to anglicize their family name, like writing "Satow" for Sato. This is another instance of self-effacement of the Japanese. In contrast to Japanese, other Asians, and Chinese in particular, are more self-reliant and self-assertive. I once knew a Siamese student who took great pains to tell his American friends how to spell and pronounce his very long and difficult name.

Japanese are often seen queueing up at a railway station to buy tickets. If some one butts in the line, chances are no one will protest, as would certainly be the case in the West. This selflessness of the Japanese people is manifested in many ways in their daily life. If a foreigner, and by foreigner I mean a Caucasian in particular, asks a Japanese passer-by the way, the latter will go out of his way to be of assistance. But often the Japanese is neither sure nor knows the way himself, in which case he will not say "Sorry, I cannot tell you," but will vaguely and in uncertain terms try to direct the foreigner to his destination.

The Japanese try to behave in an unobtrusive manner as possible; at least it is not considered good manners to assert one's self too much. Self-effacement, then, has become almost second nature with the Japanese. As a corollary to this, there is a general reluctance to assume responsibility in a given situation whenever it can be avoided. The Japanese press is a highly developed enterprise and, in fact, Japanese newspapers are renowned for their world-wide coverage and huge circulation. Yet no Japanese paper, be it the *Asahi* or *Mainichi,* or any other important daily, has a strong individuality of its own, which characterizes many of the world's leading newspapers.

Rarely does a Japanese newspaper either champion a worthy cause or crusade against anything, which is not in the best interests of society. Their editorial articles often betray their rather negative attitudes. In 1961, the government under Mr. Kishi was crumbling in the face of the nation's violent opposition to the newly concluded security arrangements with the United States. The political situation was in a turmoil. At that particular juncture, seven leading metropolitan newspapers in their editorial columns published a joint and identical statement expressing their views on the then prevailing domestic situation. Such a step is unthinkable in any other country. Why cannot a leading newspaper bravely come out with a statement of its own? Why can each and every paper not assume responsibility for expressing its own view on a given situation? But such is the extent of self-effacement, not only of a Japanese individual but also of a Japanese newspaper. Under the circumstances there is not much choice among the Japanese dailies as regards their editorial assertions, excepting those espousing a totally different cause, such as communism or a labor movement.

Apart from their innate aversion to assert one's self, the managements of newspapers are also conscious of the possible danger of losing their readers, were they to come out with something out of the ordinary. The Japanese reading public is also docile by nature and if a leading newspaper should behave a little differently from others, it will not result in promoting the sale of the paper but is more likely to alienate the readers. Also big Japanese newspapers are colossal business enterprises and more or less of anonymous entity.

After the war Japan made a new start amid paradoxical conditions to make democracy a new guiding principle. The change in outlook was accomplished not as an internal reform, but as a special situation which attended the stationing of occupation forces, and by the imposing of a new value system upon Japan. Democracy as an imported system, however, was not easily or properly grasped by a nation which lacked precedents and was haunted by the still-lingering negativism of the old ruling clique. "Freedom" as a result, was often taken to mean dissoluteness. This is not difficult to understand in the case of the Japanese who had been living for centuries under self-denial and repression and whose standard of public morals was never governed by enlightened individualism. Under the circumstances, the long-suppressed desires of the Japanese people exploded to the surface when the old value system was ideologically renounced. This relieved the people of external controls but it also found them without the necessary guiding internal controls.

At the same time respect for human rights as an important democratic precept did not foster true individualism but only helped push the people's latent egoism to the fore. Eventually personal interests emerged and the human rights concept was misrepresented as a rationalization of the now overt pursuit of exclusive personal ends and individuals sought to gratify their desires, and headlong materialistic pursuits followed in the wake of wholesale spiritual retreat. Seven years of occupation, far from fostering the healthy development of a democratic society, left the country in confusion and inertia in all fields of endeavor. Politicians place self-interests before service to the nation, and industrialists, too, often can see no further than their profits. A new line-up of capitalists is now firmly established and is working in close collaboration with politicians, and politicians of the ruling Liberal-Democratic Party now find it imperative to strengthen their ties with big business concerns if they hope to succeed in general elections. Workers, on their part, tend to be concerned too much with salaries and bonuses.

In prewar days the principles inspiring the nation were sometimes wrong but at least Japan had principles and followed them. Today principles have largely yielded to the spirit of "Enjoy today, for tomorrow who knows?" There is clearly an absence of leadership at the top and no realization of what is best in the national interests among most politicians. Generally there is a shortage of moral courage and discipline.

Elections in Japan have degenerated into a curious institution little known in other democratic countries. Japanese elections are by custom dominated by personalities rather than by policies, and the successful candidates have been those with the most local influence. Dietmen vote neither according to their own consciences nor to the wishes of their constituencies, but rather to the dictates of the party. An individual voter, too, casts his ballot not so much for a respected candidate as for one with whom the voter is personally connected in some way or other. In an election campaign for the Diet, for instance, a candidate often does not rely on each and every voter but on a certain election "boss" who undertakes to secure a block vote for the candidate. The so-called election boss, closely associated with the politician, seldom fails to get a number of estimated votes for the candidate by using his personal influence over a group of voters with whom the boss, in turn, is on close terms. It is rare that the group of voters thus approached betray the boss in the actual voting.

Politicians, once elected, are given a free hand to consolidate their positions to their advantage with a mixture of bribes and threats, openly backed by administrative power. There is an increasing tendency of late on the part of Diet members to encroach upon administrative branches of the government as a means of strengthening their position. As a result, being a Diet member is fast becoming a profession, rather than an elective post, and is even becoming hereditary in the sense that an influential politician who has assiduously consolidated his position in the constituency, can retire in favor of his son who, if he chooses to run for an election, is almost sure to be returned by virtue of his father's influence in the same electorate.

In the meantime the Diet is increasingly becoming an expensive appurtenance of the government. A member of the Japanese parliament is not only among the best-paid of world parliamentarians— he gets a fat salary over and above per diem during sessions—and he also receives various fringe benefits. He can keep up to two full-time male secretaries, whose salaries are also paid out of the national treasury. Each Dietman is allotted sumptuous quarters in close proximity to the parliament building, complete with swimming pool and other amenities. In the inflation-ridden economy Diet members from time to time decide to raise their own salaries, which is of course voted for without any opposition, thus setting an example of pay increases ahead of labor unions.

Thus being a Japanese parliamentarian is a lucrative profession, and once elected he can sit snugly on the vested interests. His concern and effort then is directed toward consolidating his position in the electorate, as well as eventually gaining a portfolio in a cabinet. In order to be successful in the scramble for a cabinet post, the most important thing for a Diet member to do is to identify himself closely with a powerful grouping in the party. Usually there are several important factions in a party and each one is headed by an influential figure who enjoys both power and wealth. This political alignment in the same party setup is particularly important for a Dietman if he is to advance in the party hierarchy. Factions are plagued by constant intrigues and recriminations. A political boss who commands the allegiance of by far the largest number of followers is likely to become prime minister in future. Then too, there is always the bargaining with other important faction bosses.

Thus a political party, though it gives a semblance of calm and unity on the surface, is always torn into factions and groups fighting for supremacy, which is reminiscent of feudal days when the country was torn into the domains of numerous war lords and internecine warfare was the order of the day. Also the relationship between a party boss and his followers is peculiarly feudalistic; the boss, in order to exact allegiance, often supports his henchmen with substantial financial aid.

This abnormal state of affairs has been brought about partly by the fact that the Socialist Party, the main opposition party, has been too impotent to challenge the conservatives and has been condemned to a place of almost permanent opposition, without the hope of ever being returned to power. During the nearly quarter of a century since the close of World War II, the Socialist Party has been at the helm of government only once, and then for only a brief period.

The Japanese Diet, then, is a strange parliamentary organ. It seems to be a perennial feature of Diet deliberations that they should be disturbed by violent tactics on the part of the opposition. All too often an opposition group resorts to physical violence such as fist-fights, when it tries to block the passage of a bill. The principle of majority rule and transfer of power between two major political parties by popular vote is, in Japan today, a thing of the past. The trend is for a political party to use the parliament merely as a machine to promote its own interest; namely for the majority party to perpetuate its incumbency and for the opposition, if not to overthrow, at least to obstruct the majority party with whatever means possible. The opposition openly lashes out at "the tyranny of the majority" and often resorts to force in order to block legislative proceedings. Obviously this cannot be regarded as anything but a direct denial of the spirit of majority rule, the very essence of democratic government.

The most salient features of the government system in postwar Japan are the strong position of the bureaucracy and the largely perfunctory role of the Diet and its impotence in formulating national policies. The role of an individual politician is that of a broker between the bureaucracy and special interests. Generally speaking, initiative in legislative matters lies not with the Diet but with the ministries which prepare the legislative proposals, and it is the government that submits them to the Diet. In recent years, it has become the practice to have important measures first cleared with key officers of the party, but the ministries still draft almost all of the important bills.

It has become the fashion in postwar years for many of the bureaucrats to go into politics. A senior government official, when reaching the position of a vice-minister or a bureau chief of a ministry, usually at around the age of 45, is almost at the end of his civil service career. He has no future because under the constitution a prime minister or cabinet minister must be a member of the Diet. In fact most of the prime ministers or cabinet ministers in recent years have been those who were civil servants in the influential ministries. The late Prime Minister Yoshida was from the Foreign Ministry, Prime Minister Ikeda from the Finance Ministry, and Prime Minister Sato is from the Transportation Ministry. Though some others have been party men; that is, those who have been politicians all along, the trend nowadays is for the ex-bureaucrats to be more successful in politics. For a senior civil servant who hails from the influential ministries, such as finance, trade, and construction, usually has connections with domestic politics and the business world, and both of these connections are needed for a successful political career.

The politician today is, to all intents and purposes, a "broker," or middleman, between the government and special interests. The special interests are represented by "pressure groups." One of the most important pressure groups in Japan is the farm lobby, which usually tries to keep the artificial price level of rice for farmers. There are also pressure groups formed by war veterans, families of the war dead, and other claimants to government pensions, who can exert considerable pressure. There are again many special interest groups in business, such as the coal or shipping industry, which try to milk the government for subsidies.

The role of the politicians can be properly

understood only in connection with the peculiar form of government in Japan. Most decisions are made by the bureaucracy, and it also controls the execution. If legislation is required, it is the ministry which prepares a draft and the draft then is approved by the cabinet and the party, and then submitted to the Diet. The ministries often decide not only what policy should be adopted but also how much weight should be attached to a certain measure and how strongly a proposal should be pushed.

In order to receive favorable consideration for its demands or wishes, a special interest group must influence the bureaucracy as well as the party. Since the drafting of most measures depends on the ministries, the bureaucrats who turned politicians usually possess the advantage of knowing how to achieve the desired results. Since a great deal of the business of pressure groups concerns budgetary appropriations, the connections between the interest groups and the politicians are very close.

It also goes without saying that large business firms and industrial concerns who want to make their influence felt, have to be on good terms with the prime minister and other important cabinet ministers in order that the latter can dispense favors or even grant financial aid to the businesses concerned in one form or other. These expectations of the business world are reflected in the size of contributions made by the firms and individuals to political parties or organizations. And since the contributions are tax exempt, the politicians need not declare them as income. A vast amount of funds has been thus funneled into political parties from business circles in recent years.

Some years ago a well-known securities firm almost went bankrupt due to a heavy loss sustained through the maloperation of investment trusts. Under the pretext of saving numerous small investors, the government resorted to an extraordinary measure of saving the firm from bankruptcy by declaring moratorium on all the debts incurred by the said securities firm for a certain period. This firm has since recovered and is going strong again. It is an open secret that the firm in question had been one of the major contributors to the funds of the political party then in power.

Generally speaking, the political parties have hardly made a positive contribution to the development of postwar Japan—their existence is largely parasitical. In present-day Japan the business world bears the chief burden of supporting these parasites. If the reigning political party wants to dissolve the Diet and hold another general election, it is to big business that the party must look for guidance; in blunt terms, to ascertain whether the business world is in the mood to pay for the cost of the election. But this interdependence in postwar years has resulted in the deviation from the proper functions of government and has hurt the legitimate interests of big business.

The curious fact is that the Japanese people, while thoroughly disgusted with the behavior of Diet members, do not seem to demand vigorously a more normal and sound functioning of their parliament. The Japanese as an individual is often a moral coward. He is not always imbued with the spirit of reform but easily resigns himself to his environment. Much of the political corruption stems from the traditional reliance in Japanese communities on personal connections in all social activities. It is an attitude that expects special, private favors in return for forming personal ties with others as distinguished from public or contractual relationships. This attitude is intense, and deeply rooted in Japan's rural communities where, for instance, supporters of a national legislator seek tangible returns quite naturally when he is appointed to a high public office.

The result is often political atrophy and poverty of leadership. The fact remains, however, that if a Diet member merely had lofty national interests uppermost in his mind, he would most likely not survive in the complicated scenes of political struggle. Such an abnormal state of affairs can only be reproduced in a country where individualism tends to take a back seat to be replaced by the concept of obedience to authority—the authority of the family, the local community, and the state.

No one, however, can deny that the Japanese political system of complex personal relationships nourished by large contributions to party funds, is entirely out of tune with the healthy development of democratic principles in postwar Japan. But while there is considerable disgust and discontent with the existing system, it is not likely that any big change will occur in the near future.

"Coprosperity Sphere," Now and Then

"TODAY I AM going to have a little talk with a salesman of transistor radios," so General de Gaulle was reported to have said just before he was to meet with Prime Minister Ikeda who was on an official visit to France in 1964. The remark attributed to de Gaulle understandably gave offense to many Japanese, but it nevertheless was a reflection on the position of Japan in the world since the end of the last war.

"The Greater East Asia Coprosperity Sphere" was the hackneyed slogan with which Japan embarked on an expansionist policy in Asia in the 1930's, and, which culminated in the Pacific War of 1941–45. In prewar years, and in fact ever since Japan was opened to the outside world, Japanese have been racially discriminated against overtly or

202

otherwise by Westerners and the Japanese have not been quite free to immigrate to wherever they wished. In the world's markets, too, Japanese were branded as odd traders and this fact, coupled with their commercial ethics and practices, were responsible for their being barred from important markets of the West. It was like a housewife trying to drive away an importunate hawker from her doorstep.

Also rising Japanese military might scared Western powers to such an extent that Japan was discreetly denied access to the sources of vital raw materials. In the meantime, Japan's population was increasing proportionately at a faster rate than at present. And owing to a severe economic depression of the early 1930's, Japan was forced to seek an outlet, both for her surplus population and for her unsold products on the Asiatic continent. At the time the Japanese, either rightly or wrongly, accused the ABCD (American, British, Chinese, and Dutch) power constellation of gradually tightening an encircling ring around Japan in order to strangle her eventually. The Dutch, by the way, were a major Pacific power in those days, ruling the far-flung island colony of Indonesia. Such in a nutshell is the background, as I see it, of the Pacific War. Thus in the immediate prewar period Japan sought, without success, to insure Asia as her own preserve, both as a source of important raw materials and as an outlet for her surplus population.

The Japanese were so frustrated with their defeat in the war that they did not feel like assuming any meaningful role in Asia for many years after the war. The Japanese in general still have the feeling that they burned their fingers in the past by intervening too much in the affairs of neighboring countries. The prevailing attitude since the war has been "Let's concentrate on rebuilding our own economy and not become involved too much in others' affairs."

There have been and will continue to be so many things to be done at home, such as the rehabilitation of the nation from the effects of the war, improvement of roads and housing, and modernization of agriculture and industry. In short, Japan has been following a policy of "economic interests first." The Japanese themselves somewhat humorously refer to themselves as being "economic animals." On many international economic issues Japan has been taking a passive attitude, examining the impact on her economy and protecting her immediate national interests. This attitude has been effective in achieving a rapid recovery and the expansion of domestic economy.

And while Japan's economy was weak and struggling to recover from the aftereffects of the war, such an attitude was more or less accepted by other countries. Gradually, as the economic accomplishments of postwar Japan have become widely recognized abroad, more is being expected of Japan in the formation of international economic policy and in the discharge of her responsibilities as one of the world's leading trading nations.

In the immediate postwar years Japan concluded reparation agreements with almost all her wartime victims—the Philippines, Burma, and Indonesia among others, and later with South Korea. These reparation payments while proving to be a serious drain on the treasury, did, at the same time, stimulate subsequent trading with these Asian countries. Japanese-made goods gradually found their way once again into these Southeast Asian countries, both in the form of reparations and in related orders.

Japanese firms and technicians are busy in India, Pakistan, and Thailand, in many cases, establishing joint ventures with local interests. Japanese department stores have been opened in Hong Kong, Bangkok, and other Asian cities with remarkable success. Representatives of various Japanese trading firms are now swarming into many Asian centers, and are engaged in their characteristic cutthroat competition among themselves, often to the delight of local businessmen, but at the expense of Japanese business interests. Thus, Japan's economic penetration of Asian countries seems at last to be gaining momentum.

Now the Japanese are again beginning to feel that Japan should once more play a leading role in Asia and in the world. Increasingly, public opinion demands this and the government gives to "Asian diplomacy" top priority on its policy program.

But is the present-day Japan really in a position to assume leadership in Asia? There are a number of factors in leadership—ideological, political, military, and economic. If Japan before the war did fill most of these requirements for Asian leadership, she is largely supplanted today in most of these areas by the United States. At present,

Washington, Peking, and New Delhi fill the gaps. Japan destroyed the power of British, French, and Dutch colonial empires in the last war, and the United States cannot quite replace them or control the chaotic political structure that now exists in Asia. What has happened is that Asia has rejected Western leadership without being able to lead herself. She has destroyed Western control, but has not yet taken control over her own national aspirations. The communists are exploiting this chaos and nationalistic yearning more effectively than the Americans are. At any rate it is evident that the United States alone, with her own resources and stock of intelligence and wisdom, cannot provide a replacement for the old system of law and order which has collapsed.

As for Japan, she has no new ideas now—not even a commonplace slogan such as "Asia for the Asiatic" to advocate. Instead she is still fumbling and groping to find her own identity. The Japanese people talk of democracy, and are convinced that they believe in it. The machinery for political democracy exists and functions tolerably well through a free press, political parties, and free elections. But something is missing somewhere. It is a split between intellectuals and the present conservative government. Intellectuals, that is, university students and professors and labor unionists, backed by the socialist and communist parties, are determined to oppose whatever the conservatives try to do. This disunity between the intellectuals and conservatives deeply affects and even nullifies Japan's international role.

On almost any given issue, including those

pertaining to foreign policy, the government gingerly supports the West, and the highly vocal intellectuals vehemently oppose it, irrespective of the merit of the issue. To cite but one example, the opposition always criticizes the administration for not vigorously pursuing its Asian diplomacy. In 1965 a project for an Asian development bank finally took shape under the auspices of the Economic Commission for Asia and the Far East (ECAFE) of the United Nations to help finance development plans of Asian countries. Japan was eminently qualified to take an active part in the bank's business and so a bill designed to authorize Japan's participation in the Asian Development Bank was presented to the Diet for approval.

The opposition Socialist Party thereupon lost no time in denouncing the bill, maintaining that by joining the bank Japan would be conniving with the "sinister imperialist motives" of the United States. They then resorted to various obstructionist tactics so that the bill could not be deliberated on during the session. As a result another special Diet session had to be convened in order to pass the legislation. Obviously such illogical opposition, which is merely for opposition's sake, is not only damaging to the reputation of Japan among other Asian nations but seriously limits the role Japan is qualified to play for many years to come.

Japan today is shorn of military power and, while saber-rattling as a means of diplomacy is by and large a thing of the past, she has no imposing military or nuclear might to awe her neighbors. At present Japan is entirely dependent on American military power to shield her against her two giant communist neighbors; namely, China and the Soviet Union.

Another important factor which prevents Japan from effectively playing her role in Asian affairs is a peculiar Japanese psychology vis-a-vis Asian peoples. The fact that Japanese bear mutual physical resemblance to other Asians does not necessarily mean that the Japanese always correctly understand the psychology of their Asian brethren. Japanese certainly do not have their neighbors' affection; but have only their grudging respect. Apart from wartime rancor and hostility which die hard, the Japanese, due to their insular character, often fail to understand the feelings of their Asian neighbors.

The Japanese people, by virtue of their feudalistic upbringing, tend to harbor feelings of inferiority to those in higher brackets of social strata, and tend to cover up their inferiority complex with feelings of superiority toward those in the lower brackets. This peculiar trait also applies when they are dealing with foreigners. The Japanese harbor an inferiority complex toward Europeans and Americans, while they tend to treat Asians with a superiority complex. This is why the average Japanese, while feeling at home in the company of Asiatics, presumably due to physical similarity, often betrays arrogance and disdain for the latter.

During the Pacific War the Japanese military in various Asian countries did not behave worse than any other foreign occupation force. In fact, some individual Japanese were so kind and obliging to the natives in the occupied areas that they made lasting friendships which continue to this day. It is not difficult to see that at the outset the Asian nations welcomed Japanese soldiers in preference to European colonizers. But taken as a whole, the Japanese occupation administration did not win the affection nor respect of the local population, largely because they failed to grasp the psychology of those over whom they ruled. The Japanese, often and quite unnecessarily, meted out harsh and inhumane treatment to the natives. This strange mentality of the Japanese toward other Asians still persists, notwithstanding the gradual improvement in the relations between the Japanese and their neighbors.

Thousands of Japanese merchants and technicians are now living in many parts of Asia. Moreover, there is a constant stream of Japanese tourists visiting such places as Hong Kong, Bangkok, and Taiwan. The Japanese are gregarious by nature and tend to keep to themselves. So Japanese residents in various Asian cities seldom mix with the local people socially, except for business purposes. Japanese are often seen playing golf, their favorite pastime, on a local golf course in large numbers—sometimes monopolizing the clubhouse facilities to the great annoyance of other club members. There is little fraternizing between local golfers and Japanese visitors. Japanese tourists are seen eating and drinking in first-class restaurants in many parts of Asia, but their behavior and table manners sometimes elicit adverse comments from other tourists and the management. The only redeeming act of the

Japanese in such cases is their notoriously known generous tipping.

Walker Hill, a mountain resort and recreation center in Seoul, built by the Korean government in an attempt to capture some of the dollars spent by American GI's, had been operating in the red for some years and it looked at one time as though the resort was financially a hopeless proposition. When, however, the peace treaty with Japan was signed and Japanese started to visit Seoul in large numbers, Walker Hill soon began operating in the black due to the free-spending Japanese, who are today the world's foremost tourists. Thus affluent Japanese, who find themselves in increasing numbers amid other Asians, are not generally respected; but more often than not tolerated because of their generosity, and perhaps welcomed because they fall easy prey to some of the shrewd local merchants.

There are surprisingly few Japanese who have ever tried to learn the Korean language, both in prewar and postwar years, though relations with Korea as Japan's immediate next-door neighbor should be of paramount importance to Japan. There have also been few Japanese who have settled in other Asian countries and devoted themselves either to business or to other pursuits. This is in marked contrast to the many European and American missionaries who settled in remote parts of Asia and made their evangelical work their lifelong career. Japanese, even in Asia where living conditions are not vastly dissimilar to their own, seldom care to settle permanently in these parts.

Japan has copied the American Peace Corps idea and has sent out contingents of youthful workers to some of the lesser developed Asian countries. These workers include judo instructors, rice farming experts, horticulturists, doctors, and nurses. But the results have not always been satisfactory. A Japanese Peace Corps worker at first feels very much at home in his new surroundings in the company of other Asians. He looks very much like other Asians and, in some cases, is almost indistinguishable from them. He can endure privation and can subsist on local meals of boiled rice and fish sauce without much ado. But the Japanese worker is often a hopeless linguist and seldom, if ever, gets to speak the language well enough to converse with the local inhabitants. He also tends to believe that the local people think and behave like his own folks back home, as the Japanese in their long history have had little contact with foreigners. In due course he is so exasperated and frustrated that he starts thinking of packing up and going back to his own crowded country.

One other point which militates against Japanese playing a greater role in Asia, and for that matter, in the world scene of today, is the paucity of Japanese politicians of international stature. While it is true that India plays an important role in Asia as a major nonaligned country, there is no denying the fact that the late Nehru, as an individual, did much to enhance the prestige of his country, thereby stealing much of the limelight and, to some extent, the leadership from some other countries. Japan has never had anyone who could speak out

211

on an international forum with the eloquence and persuasion of a Nehru or a Sukarno.

At an international meeting of Asian nations, either sponsored by the Economic Commission for Asia and the Far East (ECAFE) of the United Nations or under some other auspices, a Japanese chief delegate is often a timid and self-effacing character who dares not to speak out. If he spoke, he would most probably be reading from a prepared text which harps on vague platitudes and generalities on the given subject, and the audience yawns as a result. The text of the speech, moreover, has been prepared most probably by his subordinates after a series of discussions and consultations. The speech, therefore, is a collective and anonymous product of experts, not a straightforward utterance of the Japanese spokesman, and as such it lacks in persuasion and appeal.

In order to remedy the situation somewhat, Japanese delegates, if they are not proficient in a foreign language, are nowadays urged to speak in their own language which can easily be translated into English or French by simultaneous interpretation. A Japanese foreign minister follows this practice when giving his speech in the General Assembly of the United Nations in New York. This, however, is no solution, as a Japanese cabinet minister or other personality would still be delivering his speech from a prepared text, and translation can never convey the same feeling or impact of the original to the listener. The result is that the voice of Japan is feeble, if not inaudible, at many Asian forums and does not adequately reflect the importance of Japan as an Asian power.

212

Notwithstanding all these handicaps and short-comings, Japan has once again become the most powerful industrial country in Asia. When in the spring of 1966 the Japanese government hosted a Southeast Asian ministerial conference in Tokyo for economic development, some commentators even went so far as to allege that Japan's war-time Greater East Asia Coprosperity Sphere was being revived. But the fact that Japan has resumed her prewar position as the most industrialized nation in Asia does not in itself necessarily confer any kind of leadership on Japan in the Asian scene today.

For Japan does not wield a monopoly of technique and industry over other Asian countries, nor is Asia an exclusive preserve for Japanese products. Just as the United States is supreme militarily in Asia today, so is she a foremost trader. Britain, West Germany, and other highly industrialized countries, too, are also frantically competing in their scramble to capture their own share of the Asian market. In trade relations, Asian ties with former colonial rulers remain strong despite occasional outbursts against "colonialism." While Japan no doubt has an advantage over her rivals by reason of geographical nearness, such an advantage is largely marginal. Asian countries do not have to buy from Japan, nor are they obliged to receive technical aid from her. They want to reserve their sovereign right to choose and receive the aid which they deem most suited to their requirements.

The formation of an Asian economic community has often been talked about not only in Japan but in other countries as well. The idea sounds plausible enough and even desirable, but it simply is impractical because Asia is such a vast and disparate area and comprises mostly underdeveloped countries producing primary commodities, and whose economies are not complementary. So the concept of an Asian economic community or federation is more rhetoric than reality. Certainly it is not comparable with the European Economic Community (EEC) or the European Free Trade Association (EFTA).

It is true that in Japan the idea of Asian economic unity or solidarity has been used to justify Japanese expansion, but it now belongs to the past. Perhaps in the years to come Japan's economy will assume such a proportion that she will be in a position to dispense greater economic assistance to the developing countries of Asia. But even in such an event, for Japan to give assistance single handedly to all these nations, will not only be impractical but also not in the best interests of Japan herself.

It is possible, however, to think of an economic grouping in a more restricted geographical area, for instance, among the countries of the northern tier of Asia, such as Japan, Korea, Formosa, and the Philippines. But even that will have to be in the form of a loose economic cooperation, and will not be such a closely knit economic federation as the EEC. As for the rest of Asia, such cooperation will not be possible for many years to come, for the simple reason that the countries concerned lack in the spirit of active cooperation, and there is a great deal of rivalry and jealousy among them.

Another point which has to be borne in mind in assessing Japan's position in Asia is the very question of what is meant by the term Asia. A large segment of Japanese people suffer from the misconception of "one Asia." Asia is a vast area, the boundary of which extends from the shores of the Arabian Sea to the Pacific Ocean and from Japan in the north down to Australia. Its inhabitants are of highly heterogeneous origin. A Japanese is as different from a Burmese as a Frenchman is from a German. Similarly, an Indian is as different from a Japanese to the same extent as a European is from an Arab. Asia therefore represents plural entities. There are at least three separate ethnic and cultural groups, which can be roughly classified into Indo-Altaic, Polynesian, and Mongolian.

True, despite divergent ethnic and cultural backgrounds, Asians share something in common in their attitude toward the West. In general, their comparatively low standards of living, their past history as colonies, their difficulty in achieving industrialization by themselves—all these make them share the same problems, but this is in relative terms and again there are diversities in what appear to be their common problems.

Today Japan is torn between the desire to play a greater role in the affairs of Asia and the recognition of her limited freedom of action. Neutralist sentiment is strong in Japan and the government is reluctant to play an active role in the struggle to keep Asia out of communist hands. While realizing the growing menace of China as a nuclear power, public opinion is sharply divided on policy toward China. Generally there is strong pro-

Chinese sentiment among the Japanese. In fact there is the deep and abiding fascination China holds for Japan, mainly because of centuries-old cultural ties.

Many Japanese are beginning to assert that the American policy of containing China is not in the best interest of maintaining peace in Asia. Yet Japan is prevented from leaning too much toward coexistence with Communist China in view of her close economic ties with the United States. Obviously Japan will not be able to follow the path of de Gaulle's France, though her leaders share the belief that the problems of Asia cannot be settled without the presence of Communist China. An abrupt reversal in the country's non-recognition policy of Peking, Hanoi, and Pyong-yang is certain to disrupt the balance of power in Asia, jeopardizing the free world's position and perhaps Japan's own security.

It is obvious then that despite her industrial growth and improved stature on the world scene, Japan remains a secondary power in Asia for the simple reason that she is denied diplomatic and military initiative, and must follow the rules of the game set either by Communist China or the United States. The Japanese people and their leaders voice pious hopes to see an end to the war in Vietnam, but their desire is not matched by military, diplomatic, and other means at Japan's disposal to offer an effective solution.

The war in Vietnam, regardless of what American apologists may say, is a confrontation between American and Chinese imperialism in Asia. The United States seeks to win a victory for the defense

216

of an independent South Vietnam, and then will strive to build a "great society" in Asia, whatever that might turn out to be. Once the war is over, the United States will quietly help and encourage the uncommitted countries of Asia to form into a group or groups, politically and economically, and will provide a bulwark against the revolutionary doctrines of Peking or Hanoi. The United States may not be consciously pursuing such a policy, but that is roughly the pattern of power which is emerging in Asia.

The patent fact is that Asia's non-communist countries will not be able to hold the balance against China without Western help. It is generally realized that Asia will never be really stable unless in the long run Asians can look after themselves without falling victims to China's immense superiority in numbers. To build a self-supporting security system in Southeast Asia is a job that has to be done, for the moment at any rate, by the United States. But it is a job that will in the end have to be taken over by Asians themselves if there is ever to be a natural equilibrium in the area.

Part of the present Asian power imbalance comes from the postwar disappearance of Japan as a major military force. It is now the purpose of American policy to reactivate Japan militarily. But Japan at present is in no mood to rearm herself to the extent that she will be able to counter a Chinese onslaught single handedly. Another great difficulty in creating an Asian balance of power is the nuclear problem. If and when Japan's military power has been sufficiently built up, the problem of nuclear sharing is bound to come up, but it is problematical whether the defense of American allies can be resolved by a mere nuclear umbrella of the United States.

Japanese influence in Asia since the end of the war has been confined to the impact of a prosperous economy. The reappearance of Japan as a politico-military power might awaken suspicions which have been dormant for the last twenty years. While it is too much to say that Japan is an orphan in Asia, the fact remains that she is, after nearly a quarter of a century since the end of the war, still pretty much an isolated fortress in Asia. So if, as seems likely, the Asians cannot organize themselves to look after the military jobs of their own, it will be the United States which will have to keep large bodies of troops in the area for a long time and, who, will be forever getting entangled in Asia.

Whither Japan

WHEN IN 1952 the American occupation came to an end and Japan regained her independence, I was sent to New Delhi to open the first Japanese embassy in India. I was duly received by the late Jawaharlal Nehru, the Indian prime minister. What this illustrious statesman told me at my first meeting with him still rings in my ears.

He started by saying that after the Second World War the balance of power in the world had radically changed. "Today," Nehru continued, "a country that could be called a world power at all was one which had a huge population in the range of hundreds of millions, a vast territory, and potential material resources within its borders." Coming under this definition of world power were the United States, the Soviet Union, China, and

219

possibly India. A country like England which could only prosper by trading with overseas countries would, in the future, be reduced to a country of no great consequence, as would Japan.

This exceedingly frank, though somewhat derogatory remark, impressed me a great deal and, when pondering over the future of Japan, I often wonder if what he told me did in fact have some grain of truth.

In less than 20 years Japan has transformed a prostrate, hungry, small, overcrowded island nation meager in resources into the humming dynamo of a great industrial power. Nowhere in the world, communist or capitalist, has there been so remarkable a spurt of economic growth as in Japan in the last decade. Thus in the industrial and technological sphere Japan undoubtedly has attained big power status. Indeed, Japan is the only Oriental nation which has acquired a truly modern economy, with an abundance of scientists, educators, and technicians; with machines, the processed goods, the ships, and the capital to promote a brisk trade with nearly every country in Asia, and countries elsewhere as well.

There is a growing desire on the part of the Japanese to play a more positive role in world affairs, not only economically but politically and diplomatically. In the Diet the administration is often criticized for not vigorously promoting its "Asian diplomacy" or "U.N. diplomacy," both of which are rather ambiguous terms, so typically Japanese. Many Japanese today, especially those of the older generation, feel once again that Japan should be in a position now to play a significant role in the affairs of Asia. There is also a fervent hope entertained by a large number of Japanese that Japan could enhance her prestige and play a greater role in world affairs in the framework of the United Nations organization. Hence the cry for activization of Japan's "U.N. diplomacy."

Yet the truth is that the international image of Japan still seems strangely blurred; her voice peculiarly muted. Is this because the rest of the world does not "understand" Japan? Or is it that the Japanese themselves have been unable to define their national purpose? Before answering these questions it is important to know where Japan stands in Asia and in the rest of the world today.

The nation remains basically West-oriented in its relations with the outside world. Japanese policy-makers disavow any intentions, and see no wisdom in changing this stance—one that was imposed on Japan by the victors two decades ago but has since become a policy of Japan's own choice. Japanese claim that Japan has been interwoven too deeply in the political and economic texture of the Western community to turn back the process of integration now. In their view Japan can best provide for security and economic well-being by forming close links with the United States and the major powers of Western Europe. Moreover, the Western powers, it is held, are strong enough to shield Japan against her two giant communist neighbors. It is further assumed that Western influences are global and that their economies are vital to Japanese industries as a market and source of capital and technology.

This "Euro-American doctrine" dominated Ja-

221

pan's foreign policy in the past and still prevails today. But changes are taking place, slowly and perhaps imperceptibly, in the environment in which the doctrine was formed. First, the basic tenet of this policy is being challenged by events in Asia and also by the gradual relaxation of tension between the communist camp and Western world, the Vietnam War notwithstanding.

As Communist China builds nuclear arms and openly advocates a militant war of liberation, the shadow of China envelops the whole of Asia, from Tokyo through Rangoon to Rawalpindi. The war in Vietnam is, to all intents and purposes, a struggle between China and the United States for the domination of Asia. The question, then, is how do the convulsions in Asia affect Japan? And how does Japan propose to adjust her relations with China?

The curious fact is that Japan, shorn of her military power, does not consider China as the threat that America does, but rather respects China's growing power and prestige. Right or wrong, there is no fear in Japan of Chinese aggression. This confidence does not reflect among the people any grateful appreciation of the protection afforded by the U.S.-Japan Security Pact. Paradoxically, there are nagging fears that the very presence of American bases in Japan may actually endanger Japanese security. The only reason why the Chinese might drop atomic bombs on Japan, some even argue, would be to destroy American bases there. Realists may deride this national mood but repeated public opinion polls endorse it.

This curious complacency may be explained by

the fact that the Japanese have had a very close cultural affinity with China for many centuries. The majority of the Japanese have, at some time or other, been in China either as a tourist, businessman, or soldier, and admire the Chinese way of life, the vast and spacious territory, the relaxed mood of her people, and above all, Chinese cuisine.

In fact the history of Japan might roughly be summed up as ten centuries spent under varying degrees of Chinese influence, followed by two centuries of isolation, which was dramatically ended by Japan's emergence as an armed, industrial state bent on establishing hegemony over the Asian continent. The attempt not only failed, it left Japan facing a new China that had embarked on a program of industrialization even more ambitious than her own. Yet the Japanese in general show no sign of uneasiness and are anxious, at the moment, to enter into close economic ties with China. The sentiment of most Japanese toward China is definitely pacifist. There is little danger that Japan will go communist, but she wants to coexist with China rather than join forces with the Americans with a view to containing China.

Such attitude toward China may be justified if only because of the military position of Japan. Japan has begun to rearm and gradually take over some responsibility for her own self-defense, which American officials have encouraged. But the Japanese effort has at best been halfhearted. The Japanese, with their pacifist outlook and antipathy for nuclear war, are not likely to go so far as to build nuclear weapons and to become a foremost military power again. The staggering cost of modern armament alone precludes such a possibility in the foreseeable future. Under the circumstances, what will emerge in the Japanese-American relations in Asia is the gradual disassociation of Japan with American policy.

Over the years Japan will probably follow a policy of a de Gaullist touch and may seek to limit the presence of the United States in Asia, replacing it with Japanese influence. Yet the Japanese are not likely to speak out as strongly and as vigorously as has de Gaulle. In fact Japan would require a statesman twice as "big" as the French president to curb American reactions to such Japanese initiative to the level of anti-French sentiment in America. The Americans, on their part, will continue to assert themselves more forcibly in Asia in the face of China's expansion policy.

Thus the role of Japan in Asia, despite its growing economic importance, will have to be a secondary one in the foreseeable future, being hemmed in between the two giants—China and the United States—with little room for any independent action or maneuvering.

Looking back over the last 100 years since the Meiji Restoration, Japan's history can be divided into three distinctive periods, which also coincide with the respective reigning eras of the last three emperors. During Emperor Meiji's reign which lasted 45 years, Japan had grown from a small, unknown feudalistic Asian country to one of the foremost powers of the world. Leaders of that era were, without exception, outstanding personalities of irreproachable integrity, and served the nation with high professional competence and devotion.

In the Meiji period, the national slogan was to make Japan "a militarily strong and economically rich country."

During the Taisho period (1912–26) which ensued, statesmen also had the definite objective of making Japan even more powerful, but unlike their predecessors, leaders of the Taisho period were more interested in preserving their position of power and influence. When the Showa period was ushered in, cabinet ministers were more concerned with retaining their portfolio, without having a lofty national goal or ideal. This easygoing attitude made it easier for the militarists gradually to get the upper hand and, finally, to launch the nation into the Pacific War. Since the defeat in the war, this tendency has been particularly marked. Statesmen seem to have degenerated into professional politicians, most of whom are bent on promoting their own personal interests.

In the Meiji period, the parties and groups were identified with certain basic political conceptions, conservative or liberal, and proportionately played a more important role. Today's politicians hardly think of any policy or program as such. If any policies are formulated and propounded, it is because they can be used to get more government money, and to dispense more patronage. Politics has largely become a way of making an affluent living in some cases.

It may be that in this jet age while the world is rapidly shrinking in distance, most countries, excepting those which can truly be called first-rate powers, find it increasingly difficult to assign to themselves any significant or worthwhile role to play. In fact government dignitaries and statesmen of most other countries nowadays seem to be doing nothing more except visiting other friendly countries on official visits all the year round, reveling in VIP hospitality. Foreign ministers rush around the world's capitals, but nobody heeds them and nothing happens. There is much less chance, in the present order of the world, for a second-rate nation to become a first-rate power than was the case in the 19th century or earlier. As a matter of fact, one seldom hears of the "success story" of a nation in this latter part of the 20th century.

Similarly, a less-developed country seems forever destined to remain underdeveloped, and finds it exceedingly difficult, despite various aid received from more advanced countries, to achieve a full-fledged economic status.

Hence debility and degradation of political leaders is rather a common phenomenon, and may not be confined to Japan. Nevertheless it is true that as a result of defeat in the war, the Japanese have been reluctant to assert themselves and are still unable to define their "national purpose." Hence politicians place self-interest before service to the nation; industrialists, too, often can see no further than their profits. Workers tend to be concerned too much with "take-home" pay. Clearly there is an absence of leadership at the top, as compared with the leadership of the Meiji and Taisho periods. There is also a shortage of moral courage and discipline in most other strata of national life.

Prewar, the nation operated as one large team. And that team could usually be relied upon to

226

accomplish what it set out to do. It obeyed precise rules of conduct, in public and privately, so that it could foresee its reaction to any given problem. And above all, in prewar days, Japan was not frightened by problems and did not pretend they were unreal. No such effort and moral courage has yet been demonstrated in the defense and development of the new democratic freedom, or in the harnessing of the national will and energy to the completion of the rebuilding of a healthy nation.

Despite all their shortcomings and failings, however, Japan's leaders, in the main, adhere to a middle-of-the-road philosophy. In fact Japan's postwar industrial and social progress can be largely attributed to the nation's stable political climate and to the self-discipline and industriousness of the Japanese people. It is historically significant that no extreme revolution has ever occurred in Japan. Because of the innate conservatism of the Japanese, there is little danger that Japan will go communist. Any such course would mean economic disaster and empty rice bowls.

For some years the ruling Liberal-Democratic Party has enjoyed large popular majorities at the polls. It has also dominated both houses of the Diet. Because of the dominance of the conservatives, Japan's parliamentary system in operation is tantamount to a one-party government. By that it is meant that the ruling party is able to rule virtually without recourse to compromise or consultation with the opposition parties or the sharing of any but the least important chores. At the moment, therefore, the leading opposition party, the socialists, appear to be forever doomed to be in the opposition. However, the position of the ruling conservatives is not as secure as it appears.

In the first place the party, like any other party in Japan, is hopelessly torn into factions and groups, which are constantly waging internecine warfare and intrigue. Elections are becoming increasingly costly, which means heavier burdens on the industrialists and financiers of the country. There is general disgust with the way elections are conducted and also with the behavior of some Diet members.

In the 1965 election of the Tokyo Metropolitan Assembly the socialists managed to capture the majority, contrary to general expectations. The defeat of the Liberal-Democrats was the first since the end of the war, and was caused by the voters' disgust over pre-election disclosures of corruption and venality among the ruling conservative assemblymen. Who can foretell that such a defeat will not be re-enacted in future Diet elections? Also there is the emergence of Komei-to, the political party of the Soka Gakkai, a quasi-religious group, which no doubt will come to hold a casting vote in the balance of power of the parties in both houses of the Diet. While all these possibilities cannot be interpreted as a natural swing by the voters to the left, there is the danger that the conservatives, if left to themselves, would one day cede their position to the progressive elements.

It is sad to reflect that there has occurred no increase in comprehension regarding parliamentary processes or democratic concepts. Much of the nation's thinking is still feudalistic. For the Diet, Japan's parliament, is run mainly by elder people of prewar vintage. The younger generation, on the other hand, is becoming more individualistic, if only because it is in quest of greater material well-being. Compared with the prewar generation, the aim and purpose of life has changed enormously. Today, an individual puts himself or herself first. As a result there is a desire to break away from feudalism and the Oriental conception which puts spiritual values first and despises materialism. In postwar Japan austerity is being replaced by increasing well-being; regimentation and government controls by freedom as far-reaching as exists in any democratic society.

Naturally this trend for individualism is still crude and unpolished. It requires time to discover and develop new and permanent values. But sound individualism is a prerequisite and a basis for fostering democracy and all that it stands for. This is a hopeful sign. It may take many generations; it may still be a speck on the horizon. But the Japanese people, too, will be able to develop a truly democratic government by trial and error, given time.

The Japanese national character does include enough important traits—work discipline, the ability to relax and enjoy life, business talent, education, community spirit, unity, competitiveness, and a driving sense of obligation and guilt—all these add up to the vital compound of Japanese national activities. Indeed Japan's greatest resource is her one hundred million people. It was the drive and the ambition and the determination of her people that enabled Japan to effect such a rapid recovery from the shambles of war.

Though politicians may be reveling in the luxury of fist-fights and vote-canvassing for the Diet, there is a solid and well-organized bureaucracy comparable to that of France, and which has a century's tradition behind it. Most of the higher-echelon bureaucrats are not only honest and upright but also highly competent individuals. Thus the nation's administration is going ahead in a reasonably efficient manner.

Despite fierce competition among themselves, or perhaps because of it, Japanese industrialists are turning out products of superlative quality, and their goods are finding their way into every nook and cranny of the world. Japan has the potential to become one of the most powerful trading nations in history. The Japanese may be great exporters of goods, yet there is much more than that. Intellectual curiosity, active political minds, an artistic tradition that is both alive and good, standards of education and welfare—all this makes Japan a significant country that has not yet made the impact on the world it should, and perhaps one day will.

As Japan's industrial development proceeds, the West will be faced with a decision to lower their trade barriers against Japan in order to guarantee her a decent share of their markets. Japan, on her part, will have to abide scrupulously by commercial ethics and rules of fair trading. Japan also will be required to accept greater responsibility and economic risk for the underdeveloped countries of Asia and Africa.

But for many years it will be largely in the field of trade and industry that Japan will play a predominant role in the world. Her foreign policy will continue to be dominated mainly by economic considerations. For the reasons which have already been explained, postwar Japan is not likely to assume political leadership of Asia, let alone of the world. Racially, ideologically, and militarily, the present-day Japan simply is not equal to so grandiose a task. Rather Japan will continue to be an industrial power, and will concentrate on improving the standards of living and well-being of her people within the narrow confines of her island country.